Effortless MacBook Mastery: Lazy Tric for Maximum Productivity

Mastering MacBook Shortcuts & Productivity Hacks: The Ultimate Guide to Saving Time, Automating Tasks, and Boosting Efficiency on macOS

AXON T. GEARHART

AXON T. GEARHART

Published by **Aurora Lexicon Publishing**

CHAPTER 1: MAC HACKS 101 – ESSENTIAL SHORTCUTS EVERY LAZY USER MUST KNOW

If you want to be a **lazy yet efficient Mac user**, mastering keyboard shortcuts is the ultimate trick. Why waste time clicking around when you can perform tasks instantly with simple key combos? Here's a **complete list** of must-know Mac shortcuts that will save you **tons of time and effort**.

If you want to supercharge your learning and make the most of this book, here's a simple yet powerful trick: **grab a sticky note and write down a few key shortcuts and stick it to your screen. Practice them consistently for a few days until they become second nature.** Then, swap it out for a fresh sticky note with new shortcuts and repeat the process. This way, you're not just passively reading—you're actively embedding these shortcuts into your brain, ensuring they become a part of your skill set effortlessly!

Mastering the Function Keys (F1–F9) & Command Key – Unlock Your Mac's Hidden Shortcuts!

As soon as you open the lid of your **MacBook**, you'll notice a **row of keys at the very top**—these are your **Function Keys (F1–F12)**, and they do way more than you think! Many Mac users **never take full advantage of these keys**, but once you know how they work, they can **save you time and make everyday tasks effortless**.

So, let's **jump in and unlock their full potential!**

Function Keys (F1–F9) – What They Do by Default

These keys **control important system functions**—here's how they work:

- **F1 & F2** → Adjust **screen brightness** (F1 dims, F2 brightens).
- **F3** → Opens **Mission Control** (view all open windows & Desktops in one place).
- **F4** → Launches the **App Library** (view all installed apps in a neat grid).
- **F5 & F6** → Control **keyboard brightness** (on Mac models that support it).
- **F7** → **Rewind** media (music, videos, podcasts).
- **F8** → **Play/Pause** media.
- **F9** → **Fast-forward** media.

Pro Tip: Want to use these as regular F-keys (for software like Excel or coding)?
Hold the **"Fn" (Function) key** while pressing them OR enable traditional function keys in **System Settings → Keyboard**.

The Command (⌘) Key – Mac's Power Shortcut Key

On Windows, you use **Ctrl** for shortcuts, but on a Mac, **the Command (⌘) key is your ultimate power tool**! Here are some

must-know shortcuts to speed up your workflow:

- ⌘ + C → **Copy**
- ⌘ + V → **Paste**
- ⌘ + X → **Cut**
- ⌘ + Z → **Undo** (Mistakes? No problem!)
- ⌘ + Tab → **Switch between open apps** (Think of this as Mac's version of Alt + Tab).
- ⌘ + Space → **Open Spotlight Search** (Find files, launch apps, do calculations—instantly!).
- ⌘ + Q → **Quit an app** (Closes it completely).

Power User Tip: Combine ⌘ with other keys for **faster navigation**—for example, ⌘ + Shift + 4 takes a screenshot with custom selection!

Now that you know how **F1–F9 and the Command key** can speed up your workflow, **start using them right away!** Your MacBook is designed to be efficient, and mastering these shortcuts will make you feel like a **true power user**.

So go ahead—**test out these keys now** and see just how much faster and smoother your Mac experience becomes!

Window & App Management (For Effortless Multitasking)

- **Command (⌘) + Tab** → Switch between open apps
- **Command (⌘) + ` (backtick)** → Switch between windows of the same app
- **Command (⌘) + W** → Close the current window
- **Command (⌘) + Q** → Quit the current app
- **Command (⌘) + M** → Minimize window (Does not work if the app is in full screen mode. If the app is in full screen mode than first press escape key " esc" then press Command (⌘) + M)
- **Command (⌘) + Option + Esc** → Force quit an app

Finder & File Navigation (For Instant Access)

· **Command (⌘) + Space** → Open Spotlight Search (Find files/apps instantly)

· **Command (⌘) + Shift + N** → Create a new folder

· **Command (⌘) + Delete** → Move file to Trash

· **Command (⌘) + Shift + Delete** → Empty Trash

· **Command (⌘) + D** → Duplicate selected file

· **Command (⌘) + Option + L** → Open the Downloads folder

Text Editing Shortcuts (For Fast Typing & Editing)

· **Command (⌘) + Left/Right Arrow** → Jump to the beginning/end of a line

· **Command (⌘) + Up/Down Arrow** → Jump to the top/bottom of a document

· **Option + Left/Right Arrow** → Jump word by word

· **Command (⌘) + Shift + V** → Paste without formatting (Life-changing!)

· **Fn + Delete** → Forward delete (since Mac keyboards lack a Delete key)

Screenshot & Screen Recording (For Quick Captures)

· **Command (⌘) + Shift + 3** → Capture the entire screen

· **Command (⌘) + Shift + 4** → Capture a selected area

· **Command (⌘) + Shift + 4, then Space** → Capture a specific window

· **Command (⌘) + Shift + 5** → Open the screenshot toolbar (record screen too)

Safari & Web Browsing Shortcuts (For Speedy Surfing)

· **Command (⌘) + T** → Open a new tab

· **Command (⌘) + W** → Close the current tab

· **Command (⌘) + Shift + T** → Reopen last closed tab

· **Command (⌘) + L** → Highlight the URL bar (ready to type)

- **Command (⌘) + R** → Refresh the page
- **Command (⌘) + Shift + [or]** → Switch between tabs

Productivity & Automation Shortcuts (For Ultimate Laziness)
- **Command (⌘) + Option + D** → Show/Hide Dock
- **Command (⌘) + Option + H** → Hide all windows except the current one
- **Command (⌘) + Control + Q** → Lock your Mac instantly
- **Command (⌘) + Shift + ?** → Open macOS Help (when in doubt, ask!)
- **Command (⌘) + Option + Power Button** → Put Mac to sleep instantly

---

Bonus: Custom Shortcuts for Maximum Laziness

Go to System Settings → Keyboard → Keyboard Shortcuts to create your own custom shortcuts!

Now that you know these **lazy tricks**, you'll fly through tasks without lifting a finger (well, almost).

Pro Tips for Even More Mac Laziness

If you want to take your Mac efficiency to **the next level**, here are some **extra lazy tricks** that most users don't know about!

Universal Copy-Paste Between Apple Device

Copy on one device, paste on another!

- Just **copy** text or an image on your Mac (⌘ + C).
- Then paste it **on your iPhone/iPad** (or vice versa) with a simple ⌘ + **V** (or long-press → Paste).
- Works instantly if both devices are **logged into the same Apple ID & have Handoff enabled** (Settings → General → AirPlay & Handoff).

Lazy Level: No need to send yourself emails or messages to move text/images between devices!

Dictation Instead of Typing
Too lazy to type? Just talk!

• Press **F5 key (Function 5 key with microphone symbol) on top row to start dictation mode** anywhere.

• Your Mac will convert your voice into text instantly.

• Works in Notes, Messages, Safari, and even coding apps!

Lazy Level: Type without using your hands. Works like magic!

Two Apps, One Screen (Split View Mode)

Need two windows side by side? Don't drag & resize manually!

1. Hover over the **green full-screen button** (top left of any window).

2. Choose **"Tile Window to Left/Right Screen."**

3. Pick another app to fill the other side.

Lazy Level: No more resizing! Multitask effortlessly.

Instant Emoji Keyboard

Want emojis fast? No need to open the emoji panel manually!

• Just press **Control + Command (⌘) + Space**

• The emoji picker appears **instantly** wherever you're typing!

Lazy Level: Express emotions instantly without digging through menus.

Rename Multiple Files in Seconds
Renaming files one by one is slow! Here's the quick way:

1. Select multiple files in Finder.

2. Right-click → Choose **Rename**.

3. Use **Find & Replace** or add a sequence (like "Vacation 1, 2, 3...").

Lazy Level: Rename **100+ files** in seconds instead of manually clicking each one.

Automate Everything with Shortcuts App
Make your Mac do repetitive tasks automatically!
• Open **Shortcuts** (built into macOS).
• Create workflows like:
Auto-renaming downloaded files.
Batch-resizing images instantly.
Auto-sending pre-written emails.

Lazy Level: One click does **hours of work** for you!

Unlock Your Mac With Apple Watch

Forget typing your password every time!
• If you have an **Apple Watch**, enable **Unlock with Apple Watch** (System Settings → Touch ID & Password).
• Now, your Mac **unlocks automatically** when you're near it!

Lazy Level: No typing, no effort—just sit down, and it's ready!

Final Lazy Tip: Let Siri Handle It!

Instead of clicking around, just ask Siri!
• "Hey Siri, open Photoshop."
• "Hey Siri, turn on Do Not Disturb."
• "Hey Siri, remind me to reply to emails at 5 PM."
Lazy Level: Talk → Task Done!

CHAPTER 2: MASTERING TRACKPAD & GESTURES – SWIPE, TAP, AND CLICK YOUR WAY TO EFFICIENCY

The **MacBook trackpad** is one of the most advanced in the world. But are you **really using it to its full potential**? Most people just click and scroll, but **lazy Mac users** (like you and me) know the **hidden gestures** that make everything **faster and smoother**.

Here's a **complete guide** to mastering **trackpad gestures** so you can **navigate your Mac like a pro—without even thinking!**

---

1. Basic Trackpad Gestures (For Everyday Use)

These are the essential gestures that every MacBook user should know.

Gesture	What It Does	Why It's Useful
Click with one finger	Normal left click	The most basic function

Tap with one finger	Click (without pressing down)	Lighter, faster clicking
Tap with two fingers	Right-click (Context menu)	No need for a separate right-click button
Swipe up/down with two fingers	Scroll up or down	Smooth scrolling instead of using the scrollbar
Swipe left/right with two fingers	Go forward/back in web pages	No need to click the back button in Safari
Pinch in/out with two fingers	Zoom in or out (Safari, Photos, etc.)	Quick zoom without using the keyboard

Lazy Level: No more clicking tiny buttons—just swipe and tap effortlessly!

---

2. Advanced Trackpad Gestures (For Productivity Ninjas)

These gestures help you switch apps, multitask, and navigate faster.

Gesture	What It Does	Why It's Awesome
Swipe up with three fingers	Open Mission Control (see all open windows)	Instantly see and switch between all open apps
Swipe down with three fingers	Show App Exposé (see all open windows of the current app)	Great for switching between different files in the same app
Swipe left/right with three fingers	Switch between full-screen apps & desktops	No need to use Mission Control or swipe the Dock

Pinch in with four fingers	Open Launchpad (view all apps)	Instantly access any app without clicking Finder
Pinch out with four fingers	Show desktop (hide all windows)	Get quick access to files or widgets on your desktop

Lazy Level: No more clicking tiny icons—just swipe and pinch to control everything!

---

3. Hidden Gestures (That Most People Don't Know!)

Apple doesn't advertise these much, but they are game-changers!

Gesture	Secret Function	Why It's Genius
Three-finger drag	Drag windows around without clicking	Move windows effortlessly —just slide them with three fingers!
Rotate with two fingers	Rotate images in Preview or Photos	No need for extra buttons —just twist your fingers!
Tap with three fingers	Quick Look (shows dictionary, preview, etc.)	Check word definitions or preview links without opening new tabs!
Swipe left/ right with three fingers	Instantly switch between Spaces (multiple desktops)	Great for organizing different tasks (Work, Browsing, Entertainment, etc.)

Lazy Level: Once you master these, **you'll never want to use a mouse again!**

---

4. Customize Your Trackpad (Make It Work Your Way!)

Not all gestures work exactly the way you like? No problem— you can customize them!

How to customize trackpad gestures:

1. **Go to** System Settings → Trackpad.
2. **Click on each tab** (Point & Click, Scroll & Zoom, More Gestures).
3. **Toggle gestures ON/OFF** or change how they work.

Lazy Level: Make your MacBook **match your workflow** so you barely need to lift a finger!

---

5. Bonus Tip: Use Your Trackpad with Accessibility Features

Did you know you can use your trackpad in even smarter ways?

· **Enable Tap to Click** (System Settings → Trackpad → "Tap to click") → No need to press down anymore!

· **Enable "Three-Finger Drag"** (System Settings → Accessibility → Pointer Control → Trackpad Options) → Move windows effortlessly!

· **Use Your Trackpad as a Writing Pad** (Use Apple's built-in **Scribble feature** in Notes & Safari). If you frequently **scribble, take handwritten notes, or create digital drawings**, you will benefit from using an **external drawing tablet**. These devices can be connected to your **Mac via USB cables or Bluetooth**, allowing for **precise input and a more natural writing or drawing experience** compared to a standard trackpad or mouse.

Lazy Level: The less effort, the better!

Final Words: Become a Trackpad Power User!

Now that you know **every Mac trackpad gesture**, you can **effortlessly control your entire Mac** with just **swipes, taps, and pinches.**

No more hunting for tiny buttons or dragging windows around manually—just glide through your tasks effortlessly!

CHAPTER 3: SPOTLIGHT SEARCH LIKE A PRO – FINDING ANYTHING IN SECONDS

Do you still waste time **clicking through folders, opening apps manually, or Googling things you already have on your Mac?**

If yes, **you need to master Spotlight Search**—the **fastest, smartest way** to find anything on your Mac **instantly!**

This chapter will turn you into a **Spotlight Search power user**, so you never waste time searching again.

---

1. What is Spotlight Search?

Spotlight is **macOS's built-in search tool** that lets you:
Open **any app, file, or folder** instantly.
Find **emails, contacts, calendar events, and messages**.
Do **quick math calculations** and currency conversions.
Look up **definitions, Wikipedia entries, and stock prices**.
Search the **web** (without even opening Safari).

Shortcut to open Spotlight: Press **Command (⌘) + Spacebar**

Lazy Level: Stop **digging through folders**—just **type and find!**

---

2. How to Use Spotlight Search (Basic & Advanced Tips)

Open Spotlight: Press **⌘ + Spacebar** and start typing!

Basic Searches (The Fundamentals)

What You Want to Find	How to Search	Example
Apps	Type the app name	Safari, Photos, Spotify
Files	Type part of the file name	budget.xlsx, Resume.pdf
Contacts	Type a person's name	John Doe
Emails	Type subject or sender	invoice from Amazon
Calendar Events	Type event name	Meeting at 3 PM
Messages	Type part of a message	Hey, are you free for coffee?

Lazy Level: No more **hunting for files**—just type what you need!

Advanced Searches (Next-Level Tricks)

Spotlight is more powerful than you think! Try these advanced search techniques:

What You Want	How to Search	Example

Find files by type	kind:[file type] [name]	kind:pdf report
Find files by date	created:[date] or modified:[date]	created:today, modified:March 2024
Find specific file types	[keyword] extension: [file type]	budget extension:xlsx
Find files in a folder	folder:[folder name] [file name]	folder:Documents proposal
Find emails from someone	from:[person]	from:John
Find websites you visited	Safari [keyword]	Safari Mac tips

Lazy Level: Instantly find **exactly** what you need!

---

3. Supercharged Features You Didn't Know About

Spotlight **isn't just for searching files**—it can do **a lot more!**

Instant Calculations & Conversions

No need to open the Calculator or Google! Just type directly in Spotlight.

What You Want	Example
Basic Math	245 + 678, 45 * 90
Currency Conversion	$100 to EUR, 500 JPY to USD
Unit Conversion	12 inches to cm, 5 miles to km
Percentage Calculation	20% of 150

Lazy Level: Math done **instantly**—no need to open a calculator!

Laziest Level: To make things even easier, you can **open Spotlight Search** and then press the **F5 key** (the key with the microphone symbol) to activate **Dictation Mode**. This allows you to **speak your commands or text input instead of typing**, making your workflow even more effortless. If you want to maximize efficiency and truly embrace a hands-free experience, using **macOS Dictation** can help you get things done **faster and with minimal effort**.

Dictionary & Wikipedia Lookups

Find definitions and quick facts instantly!
- **Type any word** to see its definition → serendipity
- **Type "wiki [topic]"** for Wikipedia info → wiki Apple Inc.

Lazy Level: No need to open Safari—Spotlight brings info **to you!**

Search the Web Without Opening a Browser

Need to Google something fast? Just type in Spotlight!
- **Search Google** → weather in New York
- **Search Wikipedia** → wiki SpaceX
- **Search Apple Maps** → Starbucks near me

Lazy Level: Skip Safari—search the web right from Spotlight!

---

4. Hidden Spotlight Tricks (Only Experts Know!)

These are next-level Spotlight hacks to make searching even faster!

Use Natural Language to Search Files

You don't need to type exact words—just describe what you need!

Try this:

- Emails from last week
- Photos from last summer
- Documents I worked on in March
- Songs I added this month

Spotlight understands natural language!

Use Boolean Operators for Precise Searches

Make your searches even more specific!

Use these tricks:
- **Exclude a term:** budget NOT 2023
- **Find multiple things:** budget OR invoice
- **Exact match:** "Annual Report" (use quotes)

Filter exactly what you need!

Move Faster with Keyboard Shortcuts

Once you see a result in Spotlight, navigate quickly!

Shortcut	Action
Arrow Keys	Move through results
Enter	Open the selected result
⌘ + R	Show the file in Finder
⌘ + L	Open the full definition of a word

Lazy Level: No more **clicking**—just **press and go!**

---

5. Make Spotlight Even Better (Customization Tips!)

Spotlight doesn't have to search EVERYTHING. Customize it!

How to Customize Spotlight:

1. **Go to** System Settings → Siri & Spotlight.

2. **Uncheck items** you **don't** want Spotlight to search (e.g., News, Siri Suggestions).

3. **Prioritize important things** (like Apps & Files).

 Lazy Level: Make Spotlight **work for YOU!**

Final Thoughts: Become a Spotlight Master!

Now you know how to **use Spotlight like a pro**—no more clicking around or wasting time!

 From now on, just press ⌘ + Spacebar, type what you need, and BOOM—it's there!

Bonus Tips: Take Your Spotlight Search Skills Even Further!

You already know **Spotlight is insanely powerful**, but here are a few **more hidden tricks** that even experienced Mac users **don't know about!**

---

1. Use Spotlight to Instantly Open System Settings

 Instead of digging through System Settings, just type what you need!

Try these:

• Trackpad settings → Opens the Trackpad settings instantly.

• Wi-Fi → Jumps straight to the Wi-Fi settings.

• Night Shift → Adjusts screen colors for less eye strain.

• Bluetooth → Opens Bluetooth settings (great for connecting AirPods fast!).

Lazy Level: No more hunting through menus—**just type and go!**

---

2. Spotlight Can Find Music & Movies Instantly

Stop opening Apple Music or the TV app manually—Spotlight can do it for you!

Try these:
- **Play a song from Apple Music:** Play Bohemian Rhapsody
- **Find a movie on your Mac:** Toy Story (if it's in your library).
- **Search the App Store:** Download Evernote → Takes you straight to the Mac App Store!

Lazy Level: Skip searching manually—let Spotlight do it!

---

3. Search Inside Your Notes & Reminders

Can't find something you wrote in Notes or Reminders? Spotlight can!

Try these:
- notes groceries → Finds your grocery list from Apple Notes.
- reminder pay bills → Shows upcoming bill payments in Apple Reminders.

Lazy Level: Instantly find your important notes—without opening the app!

---

4. Convert Any Time Zone Instantly

Need to know what time it is in another country? Just type it!

Try these:
- time in Tokyo → Shows the current time in Tokyo.
- New York to London time → Converts time differences for you.

Lazy Level: No need for a time zone converter—**Spotlight does it for you!**

---

5. Check Live Sports Scores & Game Schedules

Want the latest game score? No need for Google—Spotlight has it!

Try these:
- Lakers score → Get the latest Lakers game score.
- Manchester United next game → Shows their next match schedule.

Lazy Level: Skip sports websites—just type and get updates!

---

6. Check Weather Without Opening an App

Want a quick weather update? Just type!

Try these:
- weather → Shows your current location's weather.
- weather in Paris → Get the latest Paris forecast.

Lazy Level: Stop opening the Weather app—just ask Spotlight!

---

7. Instantly Generate a Strong Password

Need a secure password? Let Spotlight create one!

Try this:

• password generator → Spotlight will suggest a random strong password.

Pro Tip: Hold down ⌘ + **C** to copy the password instantly!

Lazy Level: No need for password manager apps—Spotlight does it!

---

8. Search Inside ZIP Files Without Unzipping

Have a ZIP file but don't want to open it? Just search inside it with Spotlight!

Try this:

• kind:zip project → Finds ZIP files related to "project."

Lazy Level: No need to unzip everything—Spotlight previews it for you!

Final Words: Use Spotlight Like a Mind Reader!

Spotlight isn't just a search tool—it's **your personal assistant.** Once you **master these tricks**, you'll **never waste time searching again.**

CHAPTER 4: AUTOMATOR & SHORTCUTS APP – LET YOUR MAC DO THE WORK FOR YOU

Are you **tired of doing the same tasks over and over again** on your Mac?

What if your Mac could **rename files, resize images, move documents, and even send emails—all automatically?**

Welcome to **Automator & Shortcuts**, the ultimate **lazy Mac user's dream tools**!

With these, you can **automate repetitive tasks** and **save hours of effort** every week.

---

1. What Are Automator & Shortcuts?

Automator (For Advanced Mac Automation)

A built-in macOS app that **lets you create workflows** to perform repetitive tasks automatically.

You can use **pre-made actions** or create your own scripts.

Works great for **batch processing files, renaming, resizing, organizing folders, and more!**

Find Automator: Open Spotlight (⌘ + Spacebar → Type **Automator**)

Shortcuts App (For Easy One-Click Automation)

A newer macOS tool that **lets you create simple automation workflows** with a **drag-and-drop** interface.

Syncs with **iPhone & iPad**, so you can run automations across devices.

Works great for **quick actions** like sending messages, opening multiple apps, or auto-formatting text.

Find Shortcuts: Open Spotlight (⌘ + Spacebar → Type **Shortcuts**)

Lazy Level: With **Automator & Shortcuts**, your Mac does the work **for you!**

---

2. Why Use Automator & Shortcuts?

Here's how they save you time:

Task	Time Without Automation	Time With Automation
Renaming 100 files manually	20 minutes	5 seconds
Resizing 50 images one by one	30 minutes	5 seconds
Sorting downloaded files	10 minutes per day	0 seconds (Mac does it for you!)
Opening multiple apps every morning	2 minutes every day	0 seconds (Shortcuts auto-

launches them!)

Over time, these automations save HOURS!

---

3. Automator: How to Set Up Simple Mac Workflows

Automator lets you create workflows to automate your most common tasks.

Step 1: Open Automator
1. **Open Automator** (use Spotlight: ⌘ + Spacebar, then type **Automator**).
2. Click **New Document** → Choose **Workflow**.

Step 2: Choose an Action to Automate

Automator lets you **drag & drop** actions to create **custom workflows.**

Common Automator Workflows (With Step-by-Step Guides):

1. Batch Rename Multiple Files

Perfect for renaming images, PDFs, or music files in seconds!
1. In Automator, choose **Workflow** → Select **Files & Folders**.
2. Drag **"Get Selected Finder Items"** into the workflow.
3. Drag **"Rename Finder Items"** and choose **"Add Date or Format"**.
4. Save the workflow and run it whenever you need to rename files!

Lazy Level: Rename **100+ files in seconds!**

---

2. Convert Images to a Different Format

Need to change PNGs to JPGs? Automate it!

1. Open Automator → Choose **Quick Action.**
2. Drag **"Get Selected Finder Items"** into the workflow.
3. Drag **"Change Type of Images"** → Choose JPEG.
4. Save it and **right-click any image → Run your automation!**

Lazy Level: Convert **hundreds of images instantly!**

---

3. Automatically Move Downloaded Files to Organized Folders

Tired of a messy Downloads folder? Automate file sorting!

1. Open Automator → Choose **Folder Action.**
2. Select **Downloads folder** as the target.
3. Drag **"Filter Finder Items"** → Set rules (if file contains "invoice" → move to "Receipts").
4. Drag **"Move Finder Items"** → Choose the destination folder.
5. Save & enable it.

Lazy Level: Your Mac **sorts files for you automatically!**

---

4. Shortcuts App: One-Click Automations for Lazy Users

Shortcuts is great for creating simple, fast automations.

Step 1: Open Shortcuts App

1. Open Spotlight (⌘ + Spacebar) → Type **Shortcuts** → Press **Enter.**
2. Click **"Create Shortcut".**

Step 2: Choose an Action to Automate

Common Shortcuts (With Step-by-Step Guides):

1. Open Multiple Apps with One Click

Save time opening apps every morning!

1. In Shortcuts, click **Create Shortcut** → Click +.
2. Search for **"Open App"** → Add it.
3. Select **multiple apps** (Slack, Chrome, Notes, etc.).
4. Name it **"Start Work"** → Save.
5. Now, running this **opens all apps at once!**

Lazy Level: One click → All work apps are ready!

---

2. Send a Pre-Written Text with One Tap

Instantly send "On my way!" or "Meeting starts now!"

1. In Shortcuts, click **Create Shortcut** → Click +.
2. Search for **"Send Message"** → Add it.
3. Type your message ("I'm on my way!").
4. Choose a contact → Save.
5. Now, running this **sends the message instantly!**

Lazy Level: No typing—just tap and send!

---

3. Auto-Resize & Share Screenshots

Resize and upload screenshots instantly!

1. In Shortcuts, create a **new shortcut**.
2. Add **"Get Latest Screenshot"** → Add **"Resize Image"** (set width: 800px).
3. Add **"Share via AirDrop"**.
4. Save it → Run after taking a screenshot.

Lazy Level: No editing—screenshots are resized & shared

automatically!

---

5. Automate Everything (Bonus Tricks!)

Even more lazy automation hacks:
· **Use Siri to Run Shortcuts** → "Hey Siri, open my work apps!"
· **Schedule Mac Shutdown** (pmset schedule shutdown 23:00)
· **Create a Shortcut to Empty Trash**
· **Automate Screenshot to Google Drive Upload**
· **Schedule Do Not Disturb for Focus Mode**

Lazy Level: Your Mac now **works while you relax!**

Final Thoughts: Let Your Mac Work for You!

Now you know how to use **Automator & Shortcuts** to make your Mac do **boring tasks automatically.**

Once you set these up, you'll never go back to manual work again!

Try automating one task today and see how much time you save!

Bonus Tips: Supercharge Your Mac Automations Even Further!

You're already automating **a ton** of tasks with **Automator & Shortcuts,** but here are some **next-level hacks** to make your Mac even **smarter and lazier!**

---

1. Trigger Automations Using Hotkeys or Voice Commands

Run Automator workflows or Shortcuts instantly—without even clicking anything!

Set up a keyboard shortcut for Automator workflows:

1. Open **System Settings** → **Keyboard** → **Keyboard Shortcuts**.

2. Click **App Shortcuts** → Add a new shortcut.

3. Choose **Automator Workflow** and assign a **hotkey** (like ⌘ + Option + R).

Now, press the hotkey, and your Mac does the work for you!

Run Shortcuts with Siri:

1. Open **Shortcuts App** → Select a shortcut.

2. Click the **i (Info) button** → Enable "Use with Siri."

3. Say **"Hey Siri, run [shortcut name]"** to trigger it!

Lazy Level: Now you don't even need to click—just use a hotkey or your voice!

---

2. Set Up Automations Based on Location

Want your Mac to automatically do things when you arrive at work/home?

Example: Auto-open work apps when you reach the office

1. Open **Shortcuts** → Click **Automation**.

2. Choose **"Arrive"** → Select **your work location**.

3. Add the action **"Open Apps"** (Slack, Email, Notes).

4. Save → Now, when you arrive at work, your Mac opens all apps **automatically!**

Lazy Level: Your Mac knows where you are and sets itself up accordingly!

---

3. Automatically Back Up Important Files to iCloud or External Drive

Forget manually saving backups—let Automator do it for you!

Set up auto-backups:
1. Open **Automator** → Create a **New Workflow**.
2. Drag **"Get Specified Finder Items"** → Select important folders (Documents, Photos, etc.).
3. Drag **"Copy Finder Items"** → Select **iCloud Drive or External Hard Drive** as the destination.
4. Save & Run it **once a week**!

Pro Tip: Use launchd (via Lingon X app) to run this workflow **on a schedule!**

Lazy Level: Never worry about backing up files again!

---

4. Automatically Empty Trash & Clear Downloads Folder

Stop manually cleaning up storage—let your Mac do it!

Create an Automator Workflow to:
· **Delete files older than 30 days from Downloads.**
· **Empty Trash automatically every week.**

Shortcut Trick: Open **Terminal** and run:
sudo periodic daily weekly monthly
This cleans up unnecessary files automatically!

Lazy Level: Your Mac stays clutter-free without effort!

---

5. Schedule Dark Mode & Focus Mode Based on Time

Want your Mac to switch to Dark Mode at night automatically?

Set up a Shortcut Automation:

1. Open **Shortcuts** → Click **Automation** → Choose **"Time of Day"**.

2. Set **9:00 PM** → Add action **"Set Appearance"** → Select **Dark Mode.**

3. Save → Now your Mac **switches to Dark Mode automatically at night!**

Pro Tip: Add **"Turn on Do Not Disturb"** to avoid notifications while working!

Lazy Level: No more clicking—your Mac adjusts automatically!

---

6. Auto-Launch Websites Every Morning

Do you check the same websites daily? Let your Mac open them for you!

Use Automator to:

1. Open Automator → Select **Application**.

2. Drag **"Get Specified URLs"** → Enter your daily sites (Email, News, Work Dashboard).

3. Drag **"Display Webpages"** and save it.

4. Add this to **Login Items** in **System Settings** → **Users & Groups** → **Login Items.**

Now, every morning, your Mac opens all websites automatically!

Lazy Level: Sit down, and your workday is already set up!

---

7. Auto-Sort Screenshots Into Folders

Tired of a messy desktop filled with screenshots? Automate sorting!

Use Automator to:

1. Choose **Folder Action** → Select **Desktop (where screenshots save by default).**
2. Drag **"Filter Finder Items"** → Set Name contains "Screenshot".
3. Drag **"Move Finder Items"** → Select **a "Screenshots" folder.**
4. Save & enable it.

Now, every time you take a screenshot, it goes straight into the right folder!

Lazy Level: No more dragging files around—Mac organizes it for you!

Try at least ONE of these automation tricks today and see how much time you save!

CHAPTER 5: MISSION CONTROL & SPACES – MULTITASK LIKE A BOSS WITH VIRTUAL DESKTOPS

Are you **drowning in open windows and cluttered apps** on your Mac?

Do you **waste time clicking through windows** trying to find what you need?

Mission Control & Spaces are **your secret weapons for multitasking like a pro**—helping you organize your workspace, switch between tasks instantly, and **boost productivity without extra effort!**

In this chapter, you'll learn how to **master Mission Control & Spaces** to **work faster and more efficiently** than ever before.

---

1. What is Mission Control & Why Should You Use It?

Mission Control is a built-in macOS feature that gives you an instant overview of all open windows, apps, and desktops (Spaces).

Why it's useful:
- **See everything open at once** (no more hunting for windows).
- **Quickly switch between apps** without clicking a million times.
- **Create multiple desktops (Spaces) for different tasks** (Work, Entertainment, Projects).
- **Move apps between Spaces** for better organization.

Think of Mission Control like a "bird's-eye view" of your Mac workspace!

---

2. How to Open & Use Mission Control

Open Mission Control (4 Easy Ways)

Method 1: Swipe Gesture (Fastest Way!)
- **Swipe up with three fingers** on your **trackpad.**
- Works instantly! **Best method for MacBooks.**

Method 2: Keyboard Shortcut
- Press **F3 (Mission Control key)** OR
- Press **Control (^) + Up Arrow.**

Method 3: Hot Corner (Activate by Moving Your Mouse!)
- **Go to:** System Settings → Desktop & Dock → Mission Control.
- Click **Hot Corners** → Assign **Mission Control** to a corner.
- Now, just move your mouse to that corner to open Mission Control!

Method 4: Touch Bar (For MacBooks with a Touch Bar but not available in MacBook Air)
- If you have a Touch Bar, add a **Mission Control button** for instant access!

Lazy Level: Once you master these shortcuts, **you'll never dig through windows again!**

---

3. How to Use Spaces (Virtual Desktops for Ultimate Organization)

Spaces let you create multiple desktops to keep your work organized.

How to Create & Use Spaces

Step 1: Open Mission Control (F3 or ^ + Up Arrow)
Step 2: Move your mouse to the top right corner → Click the "+" (Add Space) button.
Step 3: Drag apps into different Spaces to organize them!

Example Uses for Spaces:

Space Name	What to Keep in It
Work	Email, Slack, Google Docs, Calendar
Browsing	Safari, Chrome, YouTube
Entertainment	Spotify, Netflix, Podcasts
Editing	Photoshop, Final Cut Pro, Logic Pro
Coding	VS Code, Terminal, GitHub Desktop

Lazy Level: No more messy windows—just **swipe between Spaces for different tasks!**

---

4. How to Switch Between Spaces (Super-Fast Shortcuts!)

You can move between Spaces effortlessly using these tricks:

1. Trackpad Gesture (Best for MacBooks!)

• **Swipe left/right with three fingers** to switch Spaces instantly!

2. Keyboard Shortcut (Works on All Macs!)
• Press **Control (^) + Left/Right Arrow** to move between Spaces.

3. Mission Control Drag & Drop
• Open **Mission Control (F3)**, then click a Space to jump there.

4. Assign Apps to Specific Spaces (Auto-Organize Windows!)
1. Right-click an app **in the Dock.**
2. Go to **Options** → Select **"Assign to This Desktop"**.
3. That app will now **always open in the right Space!**

Pro Tip: Use Spaces to keep your work and personal tasks **separate** for a distraction-free workflow!

Lazy Level: Your Mac workspace now works like a well-organized office!

---

5. Moving Windows Between Spaces (Without Closing Them!)

If you want to move a window from one Space to another, here's how:

Drag & Drop in Mission Control:
1. Open **Mission Control (F3)**.
2. Drag the window to a different Space.

Use the Dock (Quickest Trick!)
1. Click & hold an app **in the Dock.**
2. Drag it to the edge of the screen → It moves to the next Space!

Lazy Level: Easily organize your apps across Spaces without restarting them!

6. Advanced Tricks for Mastering Mission Control & Spaces

Keep Certain Apps on Every Space (For Maximum Efficiency!)

Want an app to always be visible in every Space?

Step 1: Right-click the app in the Dock.
Step 2: Go to Options → Assign to All Desktops.
Step 3: Now, this app will always be **available in every Space** (great for Music, Calendar, Notes).

Pro Tip: This is perfect for **Spotify, Calculator, or a To-Do list app**!

Disable Spaces Auto-Arrangement (So They Stay in Order!)

By default, macOS rearranges Spaces based on recent usage (which is annoying).

Step 1: Open System Settings → Desktop & Dock.
Step 2: Turn OFF "Automatically rearrange Spaces based on most recent use."

Now, Spaces stay exactly where YOU want them!

Full-Screen Apps = Automatic Spaces

Did you know every full-screen app becomes a Space?

Use "^ + **Left/Right Arrow**" to quickly switch between **full-screen apps & Spaces!**

Pro Tip: Open apps **in full screen** to reduce distractions (great for writing, editing, and watching videos).

Lazy Level: More focus, less clicking!

---

7. Bonus: Use Stage Manager with Mission Control!

Stage Manager + Mission Control = Ultimate Window Management!

Enable Stage Manager:
1. Open **System Settings → Desktop & Dock → Stage Manager → Turn On**.
2. Now, **Mission Control works alongside Stage Manager** to **group & organize apps better!**

Best Combo:
• **Use Stage Manager** to focus on one task at a time.
• **Use Mission Control** to switch between different workspaces.

Lazy Level: No more window clutter—your Mac workspace is now ultra-organized!

Final Thoughts: Become a Mission Control & Spaces Master!

Now that you **understand Mission Control & Spaces,** you can:
See all open windows instantly (No more hunting for apps).
Organize apps into different Spaces for distraction-free work.
Switch between Spaces in seconds using gestures & shortcuts.
Move windows between Spaces effortlessly (without closing them).
Try setting up Spaces today & experience how much faster your workflow becomes!
Bonus Tips: Take Your Mission Control & Spaces Skills to the Next Level!

You already know how to **organize your Mac like a pro**, but here are some **extra tips and tricks** to make Mission Control & Spaces **even more powerful!**

---

1. Quickly Close a Space (Without Exiting Mission Control)

Created too many Spaces? Here's how to remove them instantly!

Open **Mission Control (F3 or ^ + Up Arrow)**.
Move your cursor over a Space at the top.
Click the **"X" button** in the corner to close it.

Pro Tip: You can **drag & drop windows to another Space** before closing one!

Lazy Level: Keep your Spaces clean and organized effortlessly!

---

2. Assign Different Wallpapers to Different Spaces

Make it easier to identify each Space visually by assigning different wallpapers!

Step 1: Switch to a Space using **"^ + Left/Right Arrow"**.
Step 2: Right-click on the desktop → Select **"Change Wallpaper"**.
Step 3: Choose a unique wallpaper for that Space.
Now, you'll know exactly which Space you're in—just by looking at the background!

Lazy Level: No more confusion about which Space you're in!

---

3. Automatically Open Apps in Specific Spaces

Make your Mac smarter by having apps open in the right Spaces automatically!

Step 1: Right-click the app icon in the Dock.
Step 2: Go to Options → Assign to This Desktop.
Step 3: Now, whenever you open that app, it will always appear in the correct Space!

Perfect for:
· **Slack & Email** → **Work Space**
· **Photoshop & Final Cut Pro** → **Creative Space**
· **Spotify & Netflix** → **Entertainment Space**

Lazy Level: Apps open exactly where you want them—without any extra effort!

---

4. Instantly Jump to a Specific Space (Without Swiping!)

Tired of swiping through multiple Spaces to get where you need? Try this shortcut!

Open **Mission Control (F3).**
Click the **Space number at the top** to jump directly to it!

Pro Tip: If you use an external keyboard with number keys, use ⌘ + **Number Key (1-9)** to jump between Spaces even faster!

Lazy Level: Jump between workspaces instantly—like teleporting!

---

5. Enable "Reduce Motion" for Faster Spaces Switching

Want to speed up how quickly Spaces transition? Reduce the

animation effects!

Step 1: Open **System Settings → Accessibility → Display**.
Step 2: Enable **"Reduce Motion"**.
Step 3: Now, switching between Spaces happens almost instantly!

Pro Tip: This is especially useful on **older MacBooks** to make Spaces feel snappier!

---

6. Use Mission Control with Multiple Monitors for Ultimate Productivity

Did you know each monitor can have its own set of Spaces?

Step 1: Connect an external monitor.
Step 2: Go to System Settings → Desktop & Dock.
Step 3: Enable **"Displays Have Separate Spaces"**.

Now, each monitor gets its own independent Spaces, making multitasking even better!

Lazy Level: Your workflow is now on a whole new level of efficiency!

---

7. Use Keyboard Maestro to Automate Space Switching

Want even MORE control over Spaces? Use Keyboard Maestro to automate it!

Download **Keyboard Maestro** (a Mac automation tool).
Set up a macro to switch to a specific Space based on the time of day.
Example:

· **At 9 AM** → **Switch to Work Space**
· **At 6 PM** → **Switch to Entertainment Space**

Pro Tip: You can even trigger Spaces based on which app is open!

Lazy Level: Your Mac now knows when to switch Spaces—without you doing anything!

---

8. Instantly View All Windows from One App (Without Mission Control!)

Need to find a specific window from an app but don't want to open Mission Control?

Trackpad Gesture:
· **Swipe down with three fingers** → Opens **App Exposé**, showing only the windows from the current app.

Keyboard Shortcut:
· Press **F3 while holding down ⌘** → Opens **only the windows from the active app!**

Perfect for when you have 10+ windows open in Chrome or Finder!

Lazy Level: Find exactly what you need—without unnecessary distractions!

Final Words: Master Spaces & Mission Control for Effortless Multitasking!

Now that you have these **next-level tricks**, you can:
Keep your work organized with multiple Spaces.

Instantly switch between tasks using gestures & shortcuts.

Make apps open in the right Space automatically.

Reduce animation lag for a smoother experience.

Supercharge Spaces with automation tools like Keyboard Maestro!

Your Mac is now the ultimate multitasking machine!

CHAPTER 6: QUICK LOOK & PREVIEW HACKS – VIEW FILES WITHOUT OPENING THEM

Have you ever **opened a file, waited for the app to load, realized it's the wrong file, then closed it—only to repeat the process over and over?**

With Quick Look & Preview, you can instantly view files, edit PDFs, crop images, sign documents, and even watch videos—without opening an app!

This chapter will teach you **everything you need to know** to **master Quick Look & Preview** and **save hours** of unnecessary clicking!

---

1. What is Quick Look?

Quick Look is a macOS feature that lets you preview files instantly—without opening an app.

Why it's amazing:

- **Preview files instantly** (No waiting for apps to load).
- **Scroll through multiple files quickly.**
- **Edit, crop, rotate, and sign PDFs & images.**
- **Watch videos & listen to audio files—without opening QuickTime!**

Think of Quick Look as a "superpower" that lets you see inside files instantly!

---

2. How to Use Quick Look (The Basics)

Quick Look works everywhere on your Mac!

Open Quick Look (2 Easy Ways)

Method 1: Spacebar (The Fastest Way!)
1. Click on a file in **Finder or Desktop**.
2. Press **Spacebar** → The file **instantly previews**!
3. Press **Spacebar again** to close Quick Look.

Method 2: Trackpad Gesture
- Select a file → **Tap with three fingers** on the trackpad → Quick Look opens!

Pro Tip: **Use arrow keys** while in Quick Look to cycle through files **super fast!**

Lazy Level: Instant file previews = No more opening & closing apps!

---

3. Advanced Quick Look Tricks (More Than Just Previews!)

1. View Multiple Files at Once (Without Opening Them!)

Want to preview multiple files side by side? Quick Look can do that!

How to do it:
1. Select **multiple files** (hold ⌘ while clicking).
2. Press **Spacebar** → All files appear in Quick Look!
3. Click the **grid icon (☰)** to see all files in a thumbnail view.

Perfect for comparing photos, PDFs, or documents side by side!

Lazy Level: Compare files instantly—no extra windows needed!

---

2. Watch Videos & Listen to Audio Without Opening Apps

No need to open QuickTime—Quick Look can play media instantly!

Supported Formats:
· **Videos:** MP4, MOV, AVI
· **Audio:** MP3, WAV, AAC

How to do it:
1. Select a video or audio file → Press **Spacebar**.
2. The file plays **instantly inside Quick Look!**
3. Use **arrow keys to skip forward/backward.**

Lazy Level: Instant media playback—no app loading times!

---

3. Copy & Paste Text Directly from Quick Look

No need to open a file just to copy text—Quick Look lets you do

it!

How to do it:
1. Quick Look any document (Word, PDF, Notes, etc.).
2. Select text → Press ⌘ + **C** to copy it.
3. Paste anywhere using ⌘ + **V**!

Works even for PDFs—no need to open Preview or Adobe Reader!

Lazy Level: Copy text without ever opening the file!

---

4. Edit & Mark Up PDFs & Images (Without Opening an App!)

Need to make quick changes? Do it directly in Quick Look!

How to do it:
1. Open a **PDF or Image** in Quick Look.
2. Click the **Markup (⬚) button.**
3. Now you can:
- **Highlight text in PDFs**
- **Sign documents with your trackpad or Apple Pencil**
- **Crop & rotate images**
- **Add text, arrows, and drawings**

Pro Tip: You can **save the changes directly**, no extra apps needed!

Lazy Level: Instantly edit files—without opening Photoshop or Acrobat!

---

4. What is Preview & Why is it Awesome?

Preview is macOS's built-in app for viewing and editing PDFs,

images, and more.

Why it's better than third-party apps:
· **Open & edit PDFs without Adobe Acrobat!**
· **Crop, rotate, and resize images instantly!**
· **Fill out forms & sign documents digitally!**

Think of Preview as a "mini Photoshop + PDF editor" that's already built into your Mac!

Lazy Level: No need for extra apps—Preview does everything!

---

5. How to Master Preview (Hidden Features!)

1. Merge & Reorder PDF Pages (No Acrobat Needed!)

Want to combine multiple PDFs or rearrange pages? Preview can do that!

How to Merge PDFs in Preview:
1. Open a **PDF** in Preview.
2. Drag another PDF **into the sidebar** to merge them!

How to Rearrange Pages in a PDF:
1. Open a **PDF** in Preview.
2. Click **View** → **Thumbnails** (sidebar appears).
3. Drag pages to rearrange them!

Pro Tip: Press ⌘ + S to save changes instantly!

Lazy Level: No need for Adobe Acrobat—just drag & drop!

---

2. Remove Backgrounds from Images Instantly (Magic Tool!)

Did you know Preview can remove backgrounds from images?

How to do it:
1. Open an image in Preview.
2. Click **Markup (▢)** → **Instant Alpha (Wand tool ▢).**
3. Drag your mouse over the background → Press **Delete**!

Perfect for making transparent PNGs without Photoshop!

Lazy Level: Remove backgrounds in seconds—no fancy software needed!

---

3. Fill Out & Sign PDFs Digitally (No Printing Needed!)

Stop printing & scanning—sign documents digitally in Preview!

How to sign documents in Preview:
1. Open a PDF in Preview.
2. Click **Markup (▢)** → **Signature tool ✍.**
3. **Create a signature** (use trackpad, camera, or iPhone).
4. Drag it onto the document → Save!

Now you can sign forms, contracts, and invoices without printing!

Lazy Level: No more paper—just sign digitally!

Final Thoughts: Become a Quick Look & Preview Power User!

Now you know how to:
Instantly preview files with Quick Look (Spacebar).
Edit PDFs & images without extra apps.

Copy & paste text without opening files.

Sign documents digitally—no printing required.

Watch videos & listen to music without opening an app.

Bonus Tips: Take Quick Look & Preview to the Next Level!

You already know **Quick Look & Preview can save you tons of time**, but here are **even more hidden tricks** to make them even more powerful!

---

1. Convert Images to Another Format Instantly

No need for Photoshop—Preview can convert images in seconds!

How to do it:

1. Open an image in **Preview**.
2. Click **File → Export**.
3. Select a new format: **JPEG, PNG, HEIC, PDF, TIFF, or BMP**.
4. Click **Save** → Done!

Pro Tip: Hold **Option (⌥)** while clicking **"Format"** to see more hidden formats!

Lazy Level: Convert images instantly—without third-party apps!

---

2. Use Quick Look to Preview ZIP Files Without Unzipping

Want to see what's inside a ZIP file without extracting it?

How to do it:

1. Click a **ZIP file** in Finder.
2. Press **Spacebar** → Quick Look shows the contents!

Perfect for checking large ZIP files before unzipping them!

Lazy Level: No more extracting files just to see what's inside!

---

3. Rotate & Flip Images Instantly (Without Opening an App!)

Need to adjust an image quickly? Use Quick Look!

How to do it:
1. Open an image in **Quick Look (Spacebar).**
2. Click the **Markup (⃝) button.**
3. Use the **Rotate & Flip buttons** to adjust the image.
4. Click **Done** to save changes!

Pro Tip: Use ⌘ + **R** in Preview to rotate images even faster!

Lazy Level: No need for Photoshop—fix images in seconds!

---

4. Copy & Paste Images Directly from Quick Look

Need an image for an email or document? No need to open it!

How to do it:
1. Open an image in **Quick Look (Spacebar).**
2. Press ⌘ + **C** to copy it.
3. Paste anywhere using ⌘ + **V** (in Notes, Email, or Docs).

Works for screenshots, PDFs, and even text documents!

Lazy Level: Instantly copy files without opening them!

---

5. Extract a Single Page from a PDF Without Adobe Acrobat

Need just one page from a long PDF? Use Preview!

How to do it:
1. Open the **PDF** in Preview.
2. Click **View → Thumbnails.**
3. Drag the page you want **to the Desktop** → It saves as a new PDF!

Pro Tip: Hold **Option (⌥) + Drag** to create a duplicate instead of moving it.

Lazy Level: Split PDFs instantly—without special software!

---

6. Use Quick Look for Instant File Sharing

No need to open a file just to send it!

How to do it:
1. Open **Quick Look (Spacebar)** on any file.
2. Click the **Share button** (top right).
3. Choose **AirDrop, Mail, Messages, or Notes.**

Pro Tip: You can even rename the file from the Share window!

Lazy Level: Send files instantly—without opening an app!

---

7. Use Quick Look in Open & Save Dialogs

Did you know you can use Quick Look inside "Open" and "Save" windows?

How to do it:
1. When choosing a file in **Open or Save dialogs**, select it.

2. Press **Spacebar** → Quick Look previews it instantly!

Perfect for double-checking files before uploading or saving!

Lazy Level: Avoid uploading the wrong file—check first with Quick Look!

---

8. Reduce PDF File Size in Preview (Make Files Smaller!)

Need to shrink a large PDF? Preview can compress it!

How to do it:
1. Open the **PDF** in Preview.
2. Click **File → Export**.
3. Select **"Quartz Filter"** → **"Reduce File Size"**.
4. Click **Save** → Done!

Pro Tip: This works great for **emailing large PDFs without losing too much quality!**

Lazy Level: Shrink PDFs in seconds—without paid software!

---

9. Combine Multiple Images into a Single PDF

Turn images into a PDF instantly using Preview!

How to do it:
1. Select multiple images in **Finder** (hold ⌘).
2. Right-click → Open With → **Preview**.
3. Click **File → Export as PDF**.
4. Save it → Done!

Perfect for turning scanned documents or images into a single file!

Lazy Level: No need for a scanner app—just use Preview!

---

10. Use Quick Look with Spotlight for Super-Fast Searching

Want to preview files directly from Spotlight (⌘ + Spacebar)?

How to do it:
1. Open **Spotlight (⌘ + Spacebar).**
2. Search for a file → Select it.
3. Press **Spacebar** → The file opens in Quick Look instantly!

Pro Tip: Works for PDFs, images, and even Word docs!

Lazy Level: Find & preview files in seconds—no clicking needed!

Final Thoughts: Quick Look & Preview = Instant Productivity Boost!

Now you know how to:
Preview files instantly without opening apps.
Edit PDFs, images, and more inside Quick Look & Preview.
Use Quick Look in Finder, Spotlight, and Open/Save dialogs.
Convert, shrink, and merge files effortlessly!

Try out one of these tricks today and see how much time you save!

CHAPTER 7: STACKS & SMART FOLDERS – KEEP YOUR DESKTOP CLUTTER-FREE

Is your Mac desktop **a chaotic mess** of files, screenshots, and random documents?

Do you **spend too much time searching for files** buried in a cluttered mess?

Stacks & Smart Folders are the ultimate lazy tricks to keep your Mac organized—without any effort!

In this chapter, you'll learn how to **automatically keep your desktop neat, find files instantly, and organize everything without lifting a finger.**

---

1. What Are Stacks & Why Should You Use Them?

Stacks is a built-in macOS feature that automatically groups similar files on your desktop into neat, organized folders.

Why it's amazing:
• **Instantly declutters your desktop**—without deleting anything!
• **Organizes files by type, date, or tags.**
• **Updates automatically**—new files are sorted instantly.

• **Saves time searching** for scattered documents.

Think of Stacks as a "smart auto-cleaner" for your Mac desktop!

---

2. How to Enable & Use Stacks on Your Desktop

Turning on Stacks takes less than 2 seconds!

How to enable Stacks:
1. **Go to your desktop.**
2. Right-click anywhere → Click **Use Stacks**.
3. BOOM—your files instantly group themselves into Stacks!

Alternative Method (Menu Bar):
• Open **Finder** → **View** → Click **Use Stacks**.

Pro Tip: Want to see everything again? Right-click → **Uncheck "Use Stacks."**

Lazy Level: No manual organizing—your Mac does it for you!

---

3. Customize How Stacks Are Organized

Stacks doesn't just group files—it organizes them YOUR way!

Right-click on the desktop → Click "Group Stacks By" → Choose an option:

Grouping Option	What It Does	Best For
Kind	Groups files by type (Images, PDFs, Videos, etc.)	Most common setup

Date Added	Groups by when the file was added	Recent downloads
Date Last Opened	Groups by last use	Finding frequently used files
Tags	Groups by color-coded tags	Custom organization

Pro Tip: Hold Option (⌥) while clicking a Stack to instantly open all files inside it!

Lazy Level: Your desktop organizes itself—so you don't have to!

---

4. How to Use Smart Folders for Even Better File Organization

Smart Folders are "saved searches" that automatically collect files that meet certain conditions.

Why they're better than regular folders:
• **Update automatically**—new matching files appear instantly.
• **Search for anything** (e.g., all PDFs, all images, all downloads from today).
• **Create unlimited Smart Folders** for specific tasks.

Think of Smart Folders as "auto-updating file collections"!

---

5. How to Create a Smart Folder in Finder

Setting up a Smart Folder takes 10 seconds!

Step 1: Open **Finder** → Click **File** → **New Smart Folder**.
Step 2: Click "+" **(top right)** to add search criteria.

Step 3: Choose conditions (file type, date, size, tags, etc.).

Step 4: Click **Save**, name it, and choose where to store it.

Step 5: Now your Smart Folder automatically updates whenever new matching files are added!

Pro Tip: Pin Smart Folders to Finder's sidebar for quick access!

Lazy Level: Find exactly what you need—without searching!

---

6. Best Smart Folders for Instant File Organization

Here are some Smart Folders to set up for a clutter-free Mac:

1. Find All PDFs on Your Mac (Instant PDF Library)
• Create a **New Smart Folder**.
• Set **Kind → PDF**.
• Save it as **"All PDFs"** in Finder.

Now, every PDF on your Mac is in one place!

---

2. Find Large Files That Are Wasting Space
• Create a **New Smart Folder**.
• Set **File Size → Greater Than 500 MB**.
• Save it as **"Big Files"** to clean up storage!

Instantly find & delete space-hogging files!

---

3. Collect All Screenshots in One Place
• Create a **New Smart Folder**.
• Set **Name → Contains "Screenshot"**.
• Save it as **"All Screenshots"**.

Never lose a screenshot again!

---

4. Organize Files by Month Automatically
· Create a **New Smart Folder**.
· Set **Date Created → This Month**.
· Save it as **"Files This Month"**.

Great for keeping track of recent work!

Lazy Level: Smart Folders = Instant file organization without effort!

---

7. Automate File Organization with Finder Tags

Tags let you color-code & categorize files for even faster organization.

How to tag files:
· **Right-click a file → Click a color tag.**
· OR **Drag files onto a tag in Finder's sidebar.**

Pro Tip: Combine **Smart Folders + Tags** for ultimate organization!

Lazy Level: Tag files once—find them instantly forever!

---

8. Bonus Tricks for an Even Cleaner Mac

1. Automatically Delete Old Downloads

Your Downloads folder is probably full of junk—let's clean it automatically!

Open Finder → File → New Smart Folder.
Set "Date Last Opened → More than 30 days ago".
Save it as **"Old Downloads"** and delete files regularly!

Lazy Level: No more cleaning your Downloads folder manually!

---

2. Use Siri to Find Files Instantly

Too lazy to search manually? Let Siri do it!

Try saying:
- **"Show me all PDFs from this week."**
- **"Find files tagged 'Urgent.'"**
- **"Open my recent screenshots."**

Siri + Smart Folders = Instant file access!

Lazy Level: Find files without typing anything!

---

3. Move Certain File Types Automatically

Automate file organization using Automator!

Steps:
1. Open **Automator** → Create **New Folder Action**.
2. Set **"If file type = Image → Move to Pictures folder"**.
3. Set **"If file type = PDF → Move to Documents folder"**.
4. Save & enable it.

Now, images go to Pictures & PDFs go to Documents—automatically!

Lazy Level: Files organize themselves—zero effort required!

Final Thoughts: Stacks & Smart Folders = Effortless File Organization!

Now you know how to:
  Use Stacks to keep your desktop tidy—instantly.
  Create Smart Folders to find files instantly.
  Use Tags to organize files visually.
  Automate file sorting for a cleaner Mac.

  Your Mac is now always organized—without effort!

  Try enabling Stacks & creating ONE Smart Folder today—you'll never go back!
  Bonus Tips: Supercharge Your Stacks & Smart Folders for Ultimate Organization!

You already know how **Stacks & Smart Folders** can **keep your Mac clutter-free automatically,** but here are **even more hidden tricks** to take your organization skills **to the next level!**

---

1. Create Smart Folders for Files You Haven't Used in Months (Find & Delete Junk!)

  Want to find and delete old, forgotten files? Create a Smart Folder to track them!

  How to do it:
1. Open **Finder** → **File** → **New Smart Folder.**
2. Click "+" **(top right)** to add search conditions.
3. Set **"Last opened date"** → **More than 6 months ago.**
4. Save it as **"Old Unused Files".**

  Now, you can quickly delete junk files and free up space!

  Lazy Level: Let Smart Folders find forgotten files—so you don't have to!

2. Automatically Save Important Files to iCloud (For Instant Access on All Devices!)

Never lose important files—Smart Folders can sync them automatically!

How to do it:
1. Open **Finder** → **New Smart Folder**.
2. Set **File Type** → **Documents** & **Date Modified** → **Last 7 Days**.
3. Save it as **"Recent Documents"** in **iCloud Drive**.

Now, your latest documents are always available on iPhone, iPad & Mac!

Lazy Level: Work anywhere without worrying about file syncing!

3. Use Finder Tags to Highlight Priority Files (Instant Access!)

Too many files? Use color-coded tags for quick organization!

How to tag files:
· **Right-click a file** → Choose a color tag (Red, Green, Blue, etc.).
· **OR Drag files** onto a tag in Finder's sidebar.

Tagging System Ideas:
Red = Urgent Files
Yellow = Work In Progress
Blue = Archived Files

Lazy Level: Find important files instantly—without searching!

4. Find & Organize Duplicate Files (Free Up Storage!)

Macs don't automatically detect duplicates, but Smart Folders can help!

How to do it:
1. Open **Finder** → **New Smart Folder**.
2. Click "+" → **Set "Name contains"**.
3. Enter common duplicate names (Copy, Final, v2, etc.).
4. Save as **"Duplicate Files"** → Review & delete!

Pro Tip: Use a third-party app like **Gemini 2** to detect duplicates even faster!

Lazy Level: Get rid of duplicate files without effort!

---

5. Use Stacks to Keep Your Desktop Organized by Week

Want a super clean desktop? Sort Stacks by Date!

Right-click on Desktop → **Group Stacks By** → **Date Added.**

Now, files from this week stay at the top—older files automatically move down!

Lazy Level: Your desktop organizes itself every week—no cleanup needed!

---

6. Set Up a Smart Folder for Files Downloaded Today (No More Digging in Downloads!)

Tired of searching through your messy Downloads folder? This Smart Folder fixes that!

How to do it:

1. Open **Finder → New Smart Folder.**
2. Set **"Date Created" → Today.**
3. Save it as **"Today's Downloads".**

Now, all files from today appear in one place—no searching needed!

Lazy Level: Instant access to new files—without Finder digging!

---

7. Use Automator to Sort Your Desktop Automatically

Want a next-level trick? Use Automator to organize files by type, date, or keyword!

How to do it:

1. Open **Automator → New Folder Action.**
2. Set rules: **"If file type = Image → Move to Pictures folder."**
3. Save & enable it!

Now, your Mac auto-sorts new files for you—like magic!

Lazy Level: Your files organize themselves—so you don't have to!

---

8. Create a Smart Folder for Your Most-Used Apps (Skip the Dock!)

Want quick access to frequently used apps? Create a Smart Folder for them!

How to do it:

1. Open **Finder** → **Applications**.
2. Click "+" → **Last Opened Date** → **Within Last 14 Days**.
3. Save it as **"Frequent Apps"**.

Now, all your commonly used apps appear in one place!

Lazy Level: Skip the Dock—your Mac knows which apps you need!

---

9. Clean Up Your Desktop Automatically with a One-Click Shortcut

Too lazy to clean your desktop manually? Let a Terminal command do it for you!

Create a one-click cleanup button:
1. Open **Automator** → **New Application**.
2. Add **"Run Shell Script"** → Paste this command:
mv ~/Desktop/* ~/Documents/DesktopCleanup/

3. Save as **"Clean Desktop"**.

Now, double-click this app to clean your desktop instantly!

Lazy Level: One click = Instant clean desktop!

---

10. Use Spotlight Search to Find Any File—Faster Than Finder!

Forget Smart Folders—just use ⌘ + Spacebar to find any file instantly!

Try these Spotlight tricks:
- kind:pdf → Finds all PDFs.
- date:today → Finds today's files.

• tag:urgent → Finds files tagged as "Urgent."

Spotlight + Stacks + Smart Folders = Ultimate Mac Organization!

Lazy Level: Never search manually for files again!

Final Thoughts: Master Stacks & Smart Folders for a Clutter-Free Mac!

Now you know how to:

Use Stacks to keep your desktop neat—without effort.

Create Smart Folders for instant file access.

Tag & organize files automatically.

Use Automator & Terminal for even faster cleanup.

Your Mac is now cleaner & more organized than ever—without you lifting a finger!

Try enabling Stacks & setting up ONE Smart Folder today—you'll love how easy it is!

CHAPTER 8:
TIME MACHINE &
BACKUPS – SET IT
AND FORGET IT

Ever lost an important file and wished you had a backup?
Ever had your Mac crash and lost **everything**?

With Time Machine & backups, you NEVER have to worry about losing files again!
Even if your Mac dies, your files, apps, and settings can be **restored in minutes!**

This chapter will teach you how to **set up Time Machine, create backups, and keep your Mac safe—automatically.**

---

1. What is Time Machine & Why Do You Need It?

Time Machine is macOS's built-in backup tool that automatically saves copies of your files, apps, and system settings.

Why it's a MUST-HAVE:
· Restores deleted or lost files easily.
· Backs up everything—apps, documents, photos, settings, and

even your desktop.

· **Lets you recover your Mac if it crashes or gets replaced.**

· **Works silently in the background.**

Think of Time Machine as a "rewind button" for your Mac!

Lazy Level: Set it up once, and it backs up your Mac FOREVER!

---

2. How to Set Up Time Machine (Automatic Backups in 3 Steps!)

Time Machine is incredibly easy to set up—just follow these steps!

Step 1: Plug in an External Drive

· Use **a USB, Thunderbolt, or external SSD** (recommended: at least **2x your Mac's storage**).

· For **wireless backups**, use a **NAS (Network Attached Storage) or an AirPort Time Capsule.**

Step 2: Enable Time Machine

1. Open **System Settings → Time Machine**.

2. Click **Add Backup Disk** → Select your external drive.

3. Click **Use as Backup Disk.**

Step 3: Let Time Machine Work Its Magic

· Time Machine **automatically backs up your Mac every hour**!

· It keeps:

· **Hourly backups for the past 24 hours.**

· **Daily backups for the past month.**

· **Weekly backups until your drive is full.**

Now, your Mac is backed up 24/7—without any effort!

Lazy Level: You never have to think about backups again!

---

3. How to Restore Lost Files Using Time Machine

Accidentally deleted a file? Time Machine can bring it back in seconds!

How to restore files:
1. Open **Finder** and go to the folder where the file was last saved.
2. Click the **Time Machine icon (⧖) in the menu bar.**
3. Scroll through backups using the **timeline on the right.**
4. Find the file → Click **Restore!**

BOOM! Your lost file is back—just like magic!

Lazy Level: No more worrying about lost files!

---

4. How to Restore Your Entire Mac from a Backup

Replacing your Mac? Crashed macOS? Restore everything in minutes!

How to restore a full backup:
1. **Turn on your Mac** and enter **macOS Recovery Mode**:
· On **Intel Macs:** Restart & hold ⌘ + **R** until you see the Apple logo.
· On **Apple Silicon Macs:** Press & hold **Power** until "Options" appears, then click **macOS Utilities.**
2. Select **Restore from Time Machine Backup** → Click **Continue.**
3. Choose your backup disk → Select the latest backup.
4. Click **Restore** → Your Mac is back to exactly how it was!

Perfect for setting up a new Mac without losing anything!

Lazy Level: New Mac? Just restore Time Machine & it's like you never switched!

---

5. Best External Drives for Time Machine (Which One Should You Get?)

Not all external drives are equal! Here's what you need:

Drive Type	Best For	Example Models
HDD (Hard Drive)	Cheap, good for long-term storage	Seagate Backup Plus, WD My Passport
SSD (Solid-State Drive)	Fast, reliable, lasts longer	Samsung T7, SanDisk Extreme SSD
NAS (Network Storage)	Wireless, backup multiple devices	Synology DS220+, WD My Cloud

Recommended: Use **a fast SSD (like Samsung T7)** for **faster restores**!

Lazy Level: Pick an external drive & let Time Machine handle the rest!

---

6. Other Backup Methods (If You Don't Want to Use Time Machine)

Time Machine is amazing, but you should have a second backup—just in case!

Alternative Backup Options:

1. iCloud Backup (Sync Files Across Devices)
· Go to **System Settings → Apple ID → iCloud.**

• Enable **Desktop & Documents Sync**.
• Now, your files are always in **iCloud Drive**—accessible on iPhone, iPad, or another Mac!

Best for: Keeping files safe even if you lose your Mac!

___

2. Clone Your Entire Mac (For a Bootable Backup)

• Use **Carbon Copy Cloner** or **SuperDuper!** to create an **exact copy** of your Mac.
• If your Mac crashes, you can **boot directly from this drive!**

Best for: Instant Mac recovery if your internal drive fails!

___

3. Google Drive / Dropbox / OneDrive (Cloud Storage Backup)

• Use cloud storage to **back up specific folders (Photos, Documents, etc.)**.
• Keeps files **safe online** & accessible anywhere.

Best for: Protecting important work files!

Lazy Level: Use two backup methods for MAXIMUM safety!

___

7. Bonus Backup Tips (For Ultimate Peace of Mind!)

1. Set Up Time Machine to Exclude Unnecessary Files (Save Space!)

Don't waste backup space on junk files!

How to do it:
1. Go to **System Settings** → **Time Machine**.
2. Click **Options** → **Add Exclusions**.
3. Exclude **cache files, downloads, and system logs**.

Now, only important files are backed up—saving space!

---

2. Use Multiple Backup Drives for Extra Safety

Want an extra layer of protection? Use TWO backup drives!

How to do it:
1. Plug in **two external drives.**
2. In **Time Machine**, add **both drives** as backup disks.
3. Time Machine **alternates backups** between them!

If one drive fails, you still have another backup!

---

3. Back Up Your iPhone & iPad on Your Mac (Bonus Tip!)

Mac backups are great, but don't forget your iPhone!

How to back up an iPhone on Mac:
1. Connect your **iPhone to Mac.**
2. Open **Finder → Click Your iPhone.**
3. Click **"Back Up Now."**

Now, all your iPhone data is safe on your Mac!

Lazy Level: Backup everything—Mac, iPhone, iPad—with zero effort!

Time Machine & Backups = No More File Loss Ever!

Now you know how to:
Set up Time Machine for automatic backups.
Restore lost files in seconds.
Recover your entire Mac after a crash.

Use cloud & external backups for extra safety.

Bonus Tips: Supercharge Your Time Machine & Backup Strategy!

You've already set up **Time Machine & backups**, but **why stop there?** Here are **extra pro tips** to make your backups **faster, smarter, and even more foolproof!**

---

1. Encrypt Your Time Machine Backup for Extra Security

Want to protect your backups from hackers or thieves? Encrypt them!

How to do it:
1. Open **System Settings → Time Machine**.
2. Select your backup disk → Click **"Encrypt Backups"**.
3. Set a **strong password** (store it safely!).

Now, even if someone steals your drive, they CAN'T access your data!

Lazy Level: Your data stays safe—even if your backup disk is lost!

---

2. Speed Up Time Machine Backups (Stop It from Slowing Down Your Mac!)

Backups slowing down your Mac? Give Time Machine a speed boost!

How to do it:
1. Open **Terminal (⌘ + Space → Type "Terminal")**.
2. Enter this command & press Enter:

```
sudo sysctl debug.lowpri_throttle_enabled=0
```

3. Now, Time Machine **runs at full speed** instead of using "low priority" mode!

Perfect for finishing large backups FASTER!

Lazy Level: Faster backups = Less waiting!

---

3. Free Up Space on Your Time Machine Drive (Without Deleting Everything!)

Running out of space? Instead of deleting files manually, let Time Machine handle it!

How to do it:
1. Open **Terminal**.
2. Run this command:
tmutil thinlocalsnapshots / 10000000000 4

3. This **removes old backups** but keeps recent ones!

Now, you have MORE space without losing important backups!

Lazy Level: Maximize storage—without deleting backups yourself!

---

4. Set Up Remote Backups (For Extra Protection!)

Want to back up your Mac to another Mac or a NAS?

How to do it:
1. Connect to another Mac or **NAS (Synology, QNAP, WD My Cloud)**.

2. Go to **System Settings → Time Machine**.

3. Select **"Other Network Location"**.

4. Choose the remote Mac/NAS → Click **Use as Backup Disk**.

Now, your backups are stored OFFSITE—safe from theft or disasters!

Lazy Level: Your Mac is backed up—even if your external drive fails!

---

5. Use Smart Folders to Track Time Machine Snapshots

Want to see what Time Machine has backed up recently?

How to do it:

1. Open **Finder → File → New Smart Folder**.

2. Click **"+"** → Set **"Date Modified → Within last 7 days"**.

3. Save it as **"Recent Backups"**.

Now, you can instantly see all recent backup files!

Lazy Level: Find backup files without opening Time Machine!

---

6. Set a Backup Reminder (So You Never Forget!)

Using manual backups? Set up a reminder so you NEVER forget to back up!

How to do it:

1. Open **Reminders App → New Reminder**.

2. Set **"Back up Mac"** as a **weekly task**.

3. Enable **Notifications → Done!**

Now, your Mac reminds you to back up—so you don't have to

remember!

Lazy Level: Never forget a backup again!

---

7. Check Your Backup Status from Terminal (For Power Users)

Want to check if Time Machine is working correctly? Use Terminal!

Run this command:

tmutil status

Now, you'll see if backups are running, paused, or if there's an issue!

Lazy Level: One command = Full backup status!

---

8. Restore Files from Time Machine Using Terminal (For Faster Recovery!)

Did you know you can restore files without opening Time Machine?

How to do it:

1. Open **Terminal**.

2. Run this command:

tmutil   restore   /Volumes/TimeMachineDrive/ Backups.backupdb/MacintoshHD/Users/YourName/ Documents/important.docx ~/Desktop/

This instantly restores a file to your Desktop!

Lazy Level: Skip the Time Machine app—just use Terminal!

---

9. Clone Your Mac for a Bootable Backup (Time Machine + Cloning = Best Backup Plan!)

Want an exact copy of your Mac that you can boot from? Clone it!

How to do it:
1. Download **Carbon Copy Cloner** or **SuperDuper!**.
2. Select **your internal drive** → **Choose an external drive as the target**.
3. Click **Clone** → Done!

Now, if your Mac fails, you can boot directly from the external drive!

Lazy Level: Your Mac is backed up & BOOTABLE—no downtime!

---

10. Back Up iMessage & FaceTime Data (So You Never Lose Chats!)

Time Machine backs up files, but what about messages? Here's how to save them!

How to do it:
1. Open **Finder** → **Go** → **Library (Hold ⌥ to reveal it)**.
2. Copy & Save these folders:
• Messages (for iMessage history)
• Preferences/com.apple.facetime.plist (FaceTime settings)

Now, even if your Mac dies, your messages and FaceTime history are safe!

Lazy Level: Never lose important messages again!

Final Thoughts: Master Time Machine & Never Lose a File Again!

Now you know how to:

Encrypt backups for extra security.

Speed up Time Machine backups with Terminal commands.

Free up space without deleting everything.

Back up your Mac remotely or with a clone.

Restore files instantly—even without opening Time Machine.

CHAPTER 9: TEXT EXPANSION & DICTATION – TYPE LESS, SAY MORE

Do you waste time **typing the same phrases, email responses, or long messages** over and over again?

Do you wish you could **write without even touching the keyboard**?

With Text Expansion & Dictation, your Mac can do most of the typing FOR you!

You'll save **hours of effort**, whether you're writing emails, taking notes, or working on documents.

This chapter will teach you how to **type faster, automate repetitive text, and even use your voice to type hands-free!**

---

1. What is Text Expansion & Why Should You Use It?

Text Expansion (aka Text Replacement) lets you type a short shortcut, and your Mac automatically expands it into a full phrase, sentence, or even paragraph.

Why it's amazing:

- **Saves time on frequently typed words, phrases, or email replies.**
- **Reduces typing mistakes** (pre-written text = fewer errors).
- **Works everywhere** (Notes, Safari, Mail, Word, Google Docs, etc.).
- **Customizable to fit your needs.**

Think of Text Expansion as "autocorrect on steroids"!

Lazy Level: Type just a few letters & let your Mac do the rest!

---

2. How to Set Up Text Expansion on Mac (Type Faster in 3 Steps!)

Setting up Text Expansion is EASY—just follow these steps!

Step 1: Open Text Replacement Settings
- Go to **System Settings → Keyboard → Text Replacements**.
- Click "+" to create a new shortcut.

Step 2: Add Your Custom Text Expansions
- In the **Replace** column, type a short trigger (e.g., addr).
- In the **With** column, type the full phrase (e.g., 123 Apple Street, New York, NY 10001).
- Click **Done**.

Step 3: Test It Out!
- Open **Notes, Mail, or Safari** and type your shortcut (e.g., addr).
- Press **Space →** The full phrase appears instantly!

Now, your Mac types long phrases FOR you—instantly!

Lazy Level: No more typing the same thing over & over!

---

3. Best Text Expansion Shortcuts to Use Right Now

Need ideas? Here are some must-have shortcuts to make typing faster!

Shortcut	Expands To	Best For
addr	Your full address	Filling out forms
phone	Your phone number	Contact details
email	Your email address	Signing up for accounts
ty	Thank you!	Quick gratitude replies
brb	Be right back!	Messaging
sig	Your full email signature	Email responses
date	Inserts today's date	Notes & reports
faq1	"Yes, we offer free shipping worldwide."	Customer support
meet	"Let's schedule a meeting at your convenience. Here's my availability: [Insert Link]"	Business communication

Pro Tip: You can even create shortcuts for **emoji combos**!

- shrug → □♂
- happy → □
- tableflip → (╯°□°）╯ ︵ ┻━┻

Lazy Level: Let Text Expansion do the typing for you!

---

4. How to Use Dictation (Let Your Mac Type for You!)

Dictation lets you speak instead of typing—perfect for hands-free writing!

Why it's great:
· **Type without using your hands** (great for long emails, essays, or notes).
· **Works anywhere you can type** (Notes, Word, Safari, etc.).
· **Supports multiple languages** (English, Spanish, French, etc.).

Think of Dictation as a built-in "speech-to-text" assistant!

Lazy Level: Talk instead of type—your Mac does the rest!

---

5. How to Enable Dictation on Mac (Talk Instead of Type!)

Turning on Dictation is super easy!

Step 1: Open Dictation Settings
· Go to **System Settings** → **Keyboard** → **Dictation**.
· Turn ON **Dictation**.

Step 2: Set a Dictation Shortcut (For Quick Access!)
· Under **Shortcut**, choose:
· **Press Control (^) key twice** → Easiest method!
· OR Customize your own shortcut!

Step 3: Start Dictating!
· Open any app (Notes, Mail, Safari, etc.).
· Press **Control (^) key twice** to activate Dictation.
· Start talking → Your words appear on-screen!

Now, you can write an email just by speaking!

Lazy Level: Your voice = Instant typing!

---

6. Best Dictation Commands for Hands-Free Typing

Dictation supports commands for punctuation, formatting, and editing!

Punctuation & Symbols:
- **"Period"** → .
- **"Comma"** → ,
- **"New paragraph"** → Starts a new paragraph
- **"Exclamation mark"** → !
- **"Question mark"** → ?

Editing & Formatting:
- **"Select previous word"** → Highlights the last word
- **"Delete that"** → Removes the last thing you said
- **"Bold that"** → Makes text bold
- **"Capitalize that"** → Capitalizes the last word

Pro Tip: Use Dictation + Text Expansion together for even FASTER writing!

Lazy Level: Talk, edit, and format—all with your voice!

---

7. Bonus Tricks to Maximize Text Expansion & Dictation

1. Sync Text Expansions Across Your Apple Devices

Use the same shortcuts on your iPhone & iPad!

How to do it:
- Go to **System Settings** → **Apple ID** → **iCloud**.
- Enable **iCloud Sync for Keyboard**.

Now, your shortcuts work on ALL your Apple devices!

---

2. Use Dictation to Transcribe Meetings & Interviews

Need to take notes? Let Dictation do it for you!

How to do it:
1. Open **Notes** or **Word**.
2. Activate **Dictation (Control ^ key twice)**.
3. Let your Mac **listen & transcribe the conversation!**

Now, you don't need to take notes manually!

---

3. Use Third-Party Text Expansion Apps for More Power

Want more features? Try these apps!

Best Text Expansion Apps:
- **TextExpander** → Create advanced shortcuts with fill-in fields.
- **Alfred** → Automate text snippets + powerful search.
- **aText** → Cheap alternative to TextExpander.

Now, you can automate emails, code snippets, and more!

Final Thoughts: Master Text Expansion & Dictation for Effortless Writing!

Now you know how to:
Use Text Expansion to type long phrases instantly.
Set up Dictation for hands-free writing.
Automate common replies, addresses, and signatures.
Sync shortcuts across Mac, iPhone, and iPad.

Try setting up at least 3 text expansions today—you'll never go back!

Bonus Tips: Take Text Expansion & Dictation to the Next Level!

You've learned the basics of **Text Expansion & Dictation**, but here are **pro-level tricks** to **speed up your typing even more!**

---

1. Use Custom Date & Time Shortcuts (Instantly Insert Today's Date!)

 Need to type today's date frequently? Make it automatic!

 How to do it:
1. Open **System Settings** → **Keyboard** → **Text Replacements**.
2. Click "+" to add a new shortcut.
3. Set:
• tdy → Expands to **March 17, 2025**
• dtm → Expands to **Monday, March 17, 2025, 10:45 AM**
• yyyymmdd → Expands to **2025-03-17**

 Now, your Mac inserts the date format you need instantly!

Lazy Level: No more checking the calendar—just type & expand!

---

2. Make a Shortcut for Your Email Signature (Works in Any App!)

 Tired of manually typing your email signature? Automate it!

 How to do it:
1. Go to **Text Replacements**.
2. Set:
• sig → Expands to:
Best regards,
AXON T. GEARHART

Senior Software Engineer
XYZ Company
(555) 123-4567 | AxonTGearhart"@gmail.com

Now, your full signature appears in any app with just 3 letters!

Lazy Level: Type your signature in a second—no copy-paste needed!

---

3. Use Dictation with AirPods for Hands-Free Typing Anywhere

Want to dictate text while walking or cooking? Use AirPods!

How to do it:
1. Put on **AirPods** (or any Bluetooth mic).
2. Open **Notes, Email, or Google Docs.**
3. Press **Control (^) twice** to activate Dictation.
4. Start speaking!

Now, you can dictate emails while doing something else!

Lazy Level: Hands-free productivity—wherever you go!

---

4. Create Text Expansion for Canned Email Responses

Need to send the same email responses frequently? Automate them!

Examples:
• faq1 → Expands to:
"Yes, we offer free shipping on all orders above $50."
• refund → Expands to:

"We're sorry you had an issue! Please provide your order number, and we'll process your refund immediately."

• sched → Expands to:

"I'd love to schedule a call. Here's my availability: [Insert Calendar Link]."

Now, you can reply to emails in seconds—without typing everything out!

Lazy Level: Canned responses = Instant replies!

5. Use Dictation for Fast Translations (Talk in One Language, See Another!)

Need to translate something quickly? Dictate it & let Google do the rest!

How to do it:
1. Open **Google Translate (translate.google.com).**
2. Click **Microphone ⃝ (Dictation button).**
3. Speak in one language → Google translates instantly!

Now, you can translate speech into text without typing a single word!

Lazy Level: Speak your language—see it appear in another!

6. Auto-Correct Common Typos with Text Expansion

Make your Mac fix YOUR typing mistakes!

How to do it:
1. Open **Text Replacements.**
2. Set:

- teh → Expands to the
- recieve → Expands to receive
- adress → Expands to address

Now, your Mac fixes your common mistakes FOR you!

Lazy Level: Fewer typos, less effort!

---

7. Use Dictation to Write Emails Faster (No More Typing!)

Need to write long emails? Let Dictation handle it!

How to do it:
1. Open **Mail** (or Gmail in Safari).
2. Press **Control (^) key twice.**
3. Start speaking:
- "Hi [Recipient's Name], I hope you're doing well..."
4. Dictation types it out instantly!

Now, you can send emails in half the time!

Lazy Level: Talk → Email Done!

---

8. Use "Hey Siri" for Quick Hands-Free Notes & Reminders

Too lazy to type a reminder? Let Siri do it!

Try saying:
- *"Hey Siri, take a note: Meeting with Sarah at 3 PM."*
- *"Hey Siri, remind me to call John tomorrow at 10 AM."*

Now, you can create notes & reminders—without touching your Mac!

Lazy Level: Just speak, and it's saved!

9. Sync Dictation Across Apple Devices for Ultimate Productivity

Did you know Dictation works across Mac, iPhone, and iPad?

How to do it:
1. Go to **System Settings → Apple ID → iCloud.**
2. Enable **iCloud Sync for Dictation & Text Expansions.**

Now, your shortcuts & dictation settings sync everywhere!

Lazy Level: Set up once—works on ALL your Apple devices!

10. Use a Third-Party Dictation App for Even Smarter Speech-to-Text

Want even better voice typing? Try these apps!

Best Dictation Apps:
- **Otter.ai** → Best for transcribing meetings.
- **Dragon Dictate** → Advanced voice typing & editing.
- **Speech Notes** → Simple & fast dictation for notes.

Now, you can dictate faster & more accurately!

Lazy Level: Your Mac types while you talk!

Final Thoughts: Master Text Expansion & Dictation for Effortless Typing!

Now you know how to:

Use Text Expansion to type long phrases instantly.

Set up Dictation for hands-free writing.

Automate email responses, dates, and common phrases.

Sync shortcuts across Mac, iPhone, and iPad.

Fix typos & speed up writing with smart text shortcuts.

Try setting up 3 new text shortcuts & using Dictation today—you'll never go back!

CHAPTER 10: UNIVERSAL CLIPBOARD & HANDOFF – COPY, PASTE, AND SWITCH BETWEEN APPLE DEVICES SEAMLESSLY

Have you ever needed to **copy something on your Mac and paste it on your iPhone**?

Do you start an email on your iPhone but wish you could finish it on your Mac instantly?

With Universal Clipboard & Handoff, Apple devices work together seamlessly!

You can **copy text, images, and files from one device to another instantly** and **continue tasks without interruption.**

In this chapter, you'll learn how to **master Universal Clipboard & Handoff** for effortless multitasking across your Mac, iPhone, and iPad.

1. What is Universal Clipboard & Handoff?

Universal Clipboard & Handoff allow you to move content between Apple devices instantly.

Universal Clipboard → Lets you **copy text, images, videos, and files on one device and paste on another.**

Handoff → Lets you **start a task on one device and continue it on another instantly.**

Think of this as "Apple Magic"—your devices know what you're doing and help you switch seamlessly!

Lazy Level: Copy on Mac → Paste on iPhone. Start an email on iPhone → Finish on Mac. No effort needed!

2. How to Enable Universal Clipboard & Handoff

Before you can use these features, make sure they're enabled!

Step 1: Make Sure Your Devices Meet These Requirements
· **Mac:** macOS **Sierra or later**
· **iPhone/iPad:** iOS **10 or later**
· **Both devices must be signed into the SAME Apple ID**
· **Wi-Fi & Bluetooth must be ON on both devices**

Now your devices are ready to communicate with each other!

Step 2: Enable Handoff on Mac
1. Open **System Settings** → **General** → **AirDrop & Handoff**.
2. Turn ON **"Allow Handoff between this Mac and your iCloud devices."**

Step 3: Enable Handoff on iPhone/iPad

1. Open **Settings** → **General** → **AirDrop & Handoff.**
2. Turn ON "**Handoff.**"

Now, you can start a task on one device and finish it on another instantly!

---

3. How to Use Universal Clipboard (Copy & Paste Between Devices)

Copy something on one Apple device → Paste it on another. Works instantly!

How to do it:
1. Copy text, an image, or a file on **Mac, iPhone, or iPad.**
- **Mac:** Select text → Press ⌘ + C.
- **iPhone/iPad:** Long-press → Tap **Copy.**
2. Go to another Apple device.
3. Paste as usual (⌘ + V on Mac, Long-Press → **Paste** on iPhone/iPad).

Example Uses:
- **Copy text from a website on your Mac** → **Paste into Messages on iPhone.**
- **Copy a photo from iPhone** → **Paste it into a Keynote presentation on Mac.**
- **Copy a link on Mac** → **Paste it into Safari on iPad.**

Lazy Level: No need to email yourself text or photos—just copy & paste instantly!

---

4. How to Use Handoff (Continue Tasks Seamlessly!)

Start a task on one Apple device → Pick up right where you left off on another.

How to use Handoff:

1. Open an app on **iPhone, iPad, or Mac** (e.g., Safari, Mail, Notes).

2. Look for a **small app icon on your Mac's Dock or iPhone's App Switcher.**

3. Click or tap it → The app opens where you left off!

Example Uses:

· **Start an email on iPhone → Finish it on Mac in seconds.**

· **Open a webpage in Safari on Mac → Continue reading on iPad.**

· **Start writing a Note on iPhone → Finish it on Mac without copying anything.**

Lazy Level: No need to transfer files—your Mac and iPhone "just know"!

---

5. Best Ways to Use Universal Clipboard & Handoff for Maximum Productivity

Now that you've enabled these features, let's explore the BEST ways to use them!

1. Instantly Move Text Between Mac & iPhone

Use Case: Researching on Mac, but need to send text to iPhone?

· Copy **any text** on your Mac (⌘ + C).

· Open Messages or Notes on iPhone → Paste (Long-Press → Paste).

Lazy Level: No AirDrop or emailing needed—just copy & paste!

---

2. Transfer Screenshots Instantly (Without AirDrop!)

Use Case: Took a screenshot on Mac? Paste it into iPhone Messages instantly!

- Press ⌘ + **Shift** + **4** to take a screenshot on Mac.
- Copy it (⌘ + C).
- Open Messages or Notes on **iPhone** → **Paste**.

Lazy Level: Skip the AirDrop step—just copy & paste!

---

3. Start Reading an Article on Mac, Finish on iPhone

Use Case: Found an interesting article? Switch devices instantly!

- Open **Safari on Mac** → Browse an article.
- Open **iPhone** → **App Switcher (Swipe Up or Double-Click Home Button).**
- Tap the **Safari Handoff icon** → The article opens instantly!

Lazy Level: No searching—your Mac & iPhone sync automatically!

---

4. Drag & Drop Files Between Mac & iPad Using Universal Clipboard

Use Case: Working on a Keynote presentation? Move images FAST!

- Copy an **image or file** on Mac (⌘ + C).
- Open **Keynote on iPad** → Tap & Paste.

Lazy Level: No AirDrop needed—just copy & paste across devices!

---

5. Continue Typing Emails from iPhone to Mac Instantly

Use Case: Started an email on iPhone, but want to finish on Mac?

• Open **Mail on iPhone** → Start typing an email.

• Open **Mac** → **Click the Mail icon in the Dock (with a small iPhone icon).**

• Your draft opens exactly where you left off!

Lazy Level: Start typing anywhere—your email follows you!

---

6. Bonus Tips for Mastering Universal Clipboard & Handoff

1. Use Handoff to Copy Passwords from iPhone to Mac

Need a password saved in iPhone Keychain? Copy & paste it to Mac!

How to do it:

1. Open **Settings** → **Passwords** on iPhone.

2. Tap a saved password → **Copy**.

3. Paste into the Mac login field (⌘ + V).

Now, no need to type long passwords manually!

Lazy Level: Copy & paste passwords securely between devices!

---

2. Use Handoff to Quickly Move Phone Calls Between Mac & iPhone

On a call on iPhone? Move it to Mac instantly!

How to do it:

1. Answer a call on iPhone.

2. Click **Handoff icon on Mac** (top right).

3. The call transfers seamlessly to your Mac!

Perfect for work calls when switching devices!

Lazy Level: No call drop—just move the call to Mac & continue talking!

Final Thoughts: Master Universal Clipboard & Handoff for Seamless Apple Multitasking!

Now you know how to:
Copy & paste text, images, and files between Apple devices.
Start tasks on one device and finish on another instantly.
Use Handoff to move Safari, Mail, Notes, and more.
Transfer screenshots, emails, and passwords effortlessly.

Try copying text on your Mac & pasting it on your iPhone NOW—it's game-changing!
Bonus Tips: Master Universal Clipboard & Handoff Like a Pro!

You've already learned the **magic of Universal Clipboard & Handoff**, but here are **extra power-user tricks** to make your Mac and iPhone work even better together!

---

1. Copy & Paste Phone Numbers from Mac to iPhone (Instant Dialing!)

Ever found a phone number on your Mac but don't want to type it into your iPhone? Just copy & paste it!

How to do it:
1. Highlight a phone number on your **Mac** (Safari, Notes, Email, etc.).
2. Press ⌘ + **C (Copy).**

3. Open the **Phone app on iPhone** → Long-press in the dialer → Tap **Paste**.

Now, you can dial numbers instantly—without typing!

Lazy Level: Copy a number on Mac → Call on iPhone in seconds!

---

2. Open Directions on Mac & Instantly Continue on iPhone

Looking up directions on your Mac? Open them on iPhone instantly!

How to do it:
1. Open **Apple Maps on Mac** → Search for a location.
2. Click **Directions** → **Choose iPhone from the "Share" menu.**
3. Your iPhone **instantly opens Maps** with the same directions.

Now, no need to re-enter addresses on your iPhone!

Lazy Level: Plan on Mac → Navigate on iPhone in seconds!

---

3. Quickly Transfer Images Between iPhone & Mac Without AirDrop

Want to send a photo from your iPhone to Mac super fast? Just copy & paste it!

How to do it:
1. Open **Photos on iPhone** → Select an image.
2. Tap **Share** → **Copy Photo**.
3. Go to **Mac** → **Paste (⌘ + V) into Notes, Messages, or Keynote.**

No need to use AirDrop—just copy & paste across devices!

Lazy Level: Move images instantly without extra steps!

---

4. Copy & Paste Entire Files Between Mac & iPad

Universal Clipboard isn't just for text—it works for files too!

How to do it:
1. On **Mac**, select a file in **Finder**.
2. Press ⌘ + **C (Copy)**.
3. Open **Files app on iPad** → Long-press → Tap **Paste**.

Now, files move seamlessly between devices!

Lazy Level: No need for AirDrop—just copy & paste files!

---

5. Start Writing an iMessage on Mac, Finish on iPhone Instantly

Want to continue texting while leaving your desk? Let Handoff do the work!

How to do it:
1. Open **Messages on Mac** → Start typing a message.
2. Open **iPhone** → **App Switcher (Swipe up or Double-Click Home Button)**.
3. Tap the **Handoff icon** → Your draft is waiting!

Perfect for replying to messages across devices!

Lazy Level: Start anywhere, finish anywhere—no effort needed!

---

6. Move Photos from iPhone to Mac While Editing (Without

AirDrop!)

Working on a project on Mac but took a great photo on iPhone? Copy it over instantly!

How to do it:
1. Open **Photos on iPhone** → Select an image.
2. Tap **Copy Photo.**
3. Open **Photoshop, Pages, or Notes on Mac** → Press ⌘ + **V** **(Paste).**

Now, your images move instantly between devices!

Lazy Level: No extra steps—just copy & paste!

---

7. Use Handoff to Copy Links Between Mac & iPhone Instantly

Found a great article on Mac? Open it instantly on iPhone!

How to do it:
1. Copy the **URL** from Safari on Mac (⌘ + C).
2. Open Safari on **iPhone** → Long-Press the Address Bar → Tap **Paste & Go.**

No need to retype links—just copy & paste!

Lazy Level: Browse on Mac → Instantly open on iPhone!

---

8. Start an Online Form on iPhone, Finish It on Mac

Filling out a long form on iPhone? Move it to Mac instantly!

How to do it:
1. Start typing in **Safari on iPhone** (checkout, login, etc.).

2. Open **Safari on Mac** → Click the **Handoff icon in the Dock.**

3. The same page opens with your info filled in!

Now, you can finish on Mac without losing progress!

Lazy Level: No need to start over—just pick up where you left off!

---

9. Share Clipboard Between Mac & iPad for Drawing & Notes

If you don't have a drawing tablet than use your iPad as a drawing tablet and paste sketches into Mac instantly!

How to do it:

1. Open **Notes on iPad** → Sketch using Apple Pencil.

2. Select the drawing → Tap **Copy**.

3. Go to **Mac Notes** → **Paste (⌘ + V).**

Now, hand-drawn notes transfer instantly between devices!

Lazy Level: Draw on iPad → Paste into Mac instantly!

---

10. Quickly Open Recent Documents from iPhone to Mac

Opened a file on iPhone? Continue editing on Mac instantly!

How to do it:

1. Open **Files app on iPhone** → Recent files.

2. Open **Mac** → **Finder** → **Recent Items.**

3. Your file is ready to continue working on!

Now, your documents are accessible across all devices instantly!

Lazy Level: Your Mac & iPhone are perfectly in sync!

Final Thoughts: Master Universal Clipboard & Handoff for Effortless Multitasking!

Now you know how to:

Copy & paste text, images, and files between devices.

Use Handoff to continue emails, texts, and web browsing seamlessly.

Open directions, passwords, and links instantly across devices.

Move photos, documents, and sketches effortlessly.

Try copying something on your Mac & pasting it on iPhone NOW—it's game-changing!

CHAPTER 11: SPOTLIGHT SEARCH PRO HACKS – FIND ANYTHING INSTANTLY ON YOUR MAC

Do you still waste time clicking through folders, hunting for files, or opening apps manually?

Do you open Safari every time you need to look up a simple calculation or definition?

Spotlight Search is your Mac's built-in superpower that helps you find anything instantly!

It can **open apps, search documents, find emails, do calculations, look up dictionary definitions, check the weather, and so much more—all in seconds!**

This chapter will teach you **all the Spotlight Search hacks you need to navigate your Mac like a pro!**

---

1. What is Spotlight Search & Why Should You Use It?

Spotlight Search is macOS's built-in search tool that lets you find anything on your Mac instantly.

Why it's amazing:
- **Opens apps, files, folders, and system settings in seconds.**
- **Searches emails, contacts, messages, and calendar events.**
- **Performs instant calculations & conversions.**
- **Finds definitions, stock prices, sports scores, and weather updates.**
- **Searches the web without opening a browser.**

Think of Spotlight as your Mac's "Google Search" but for EVERYTHING!

Lazy Level: No more digging through Finder—just type & find!

---

2. How to Open & Use Spotlight Search

Opening Spotlight is SUPER easy!

Three Ways to Open Spotlight:
1. **Press ⌘ + Spacebar (FASTEST way!).**
2. **Click the ⬚ Spotlight icon** in the top-right menu bar.
3. **Use Siri** → Say: "Search for [anything] on my Mac."

Now, just start typing what you're looking for!

Lazy Level: Forget clicking through folders—Spotlight finds everything!

---

3. Use Spotlight to Instantly Open Apps & Files

No more searching through Launchpad or Finder—Spotlight opens anything instantly!

How to do it:

- **Type the name of any app** → Press **Enter** to open it.
- Example: Safari → Press **Enter** → Safari opens instantly!
- **Type a file name** → Press **Enter** to open it.
- Example: resume.pdf → Open your resume in seconds!

Pro Tip:
- **Use arrow keys** to navigate results faster.
- **Press ⌘ + R** on a file result to **see its location in Finder!**

Lazy Level: Open anything in seconds—no clicking needed!

---

4. Use Spotlight for Instant Calculations & Conversions

Spotlight replaces your calculator & unit converter!

How to do it:
- **Basic Math:**
- 245 + 678 → Shows the result instantly!
- 50 * 32 → Calculates it without opening an app!
- **Currency Conversions:**
- $100 to EUR → Converts USD to Euros!
- 500 JPY to USD → Converts Yen to Dollars!
- **Unit Conversions:**
- 12 inches to cm → Converts instantly!
- 5 miles to km → No need for Google!

Perfect for quick math & currency conversions!

Lazy Level: Do calculations without even touching a calculator!

---

5. Use Spotlight for Dictionary Definitions & Wikipedia Lookups

Want to define a word or look up something on Wikipedia? Just Spotlight it!

How to do it:
- **Type any word** → See its definition instantly!
- Example: serendipity → Shows the dictionary definition.
- **Type wiki [topic]** → Searches Wikipedia.
- Example: wiki Steve Jobs → Opens his Wikipedia page!

No need to open Safari—Spotlight finds the info instantly!

Lazy Level: Instant definitions & Wikipedia results—without a browser!

---

6. Search Emails, Messages, & Contacts Instantly

Stop scrolling through Mail & Messages—Spotlight finds them instantly!

How to do it:
- **Find emails from someone:**
- from:John → Shows all emails from John.
- **Find a message in iMessage:**
- Hey, are you free for coffee? → Finds the exact message.
- **Find contacts:**
- John Doe → Shows their phone number, email, & address.

No more digging through apps—Spotlight finds conversations instantly!

Lazy Level: Stop scrolling—just search & find instantly!

---

7. Open System Settings & Control Your Mac

No more clicking through settings—Spotlight takes you straight there!

How to do it:
- **Adjust settings quickly:**
- Trackpad settings → Opens Trackpad settings.
- Wi-Fi → Opens Wi-Fi settings instantly.
- **Launch system apps instantly:**
- Activity Monitor → Open it instantly!
- Bluetooth → Jump to Bluetooth settings!

Now, adjusting your Mac's settings is easier than ever!

Lazy Level: No more digging through System Settings—just type & go!

---

8. Bonus Pro Tips for Mastering Spotlight Search

1. Use Boolean Operators for Precise Searches

Want more advanced search tricks? Use these!

How to do it:
- **Exclude a word:** budget NOT 2023
- **Find multiple things:** budget OR invoice
- **Exact match:** "Annual Report" (use quotes)

Get super specific with your searches!

Lazy Level: Find exactly what you need—instantly!

---

2. Quickly See File Previews Without Opening Them

Need to check a file before opening it? Preview it with Quick Look!

How to do it:
1. Search for a file in Spotlight.
2. Press **Spacebar** to see a quick preview.

Perfect for checking PDFs, images, and text files FAST!

Lazy Level: No need to open files—just preview & go!

---

3. Search the Web Without Opening a Browser

Skip Google—search the web straight from Spotlight!

How to do it:
- weather in New York → Shows the latest weather.
- Google Mac shortcuts → Opens a Google search in Safari.
- news → Shows the latest news headlines.

Now, you don't even need to open Safari for simple searches!

Lazy Level: Find info online—without a browser!

---

4. Use Spotlight as an App Launcher (Faster Than Dock & Launchpad!)

Ditch the Dock—launch apps in seconds!

How to do it:
1. Press ⌘ + Spacebar.
2. Type an app's name → Press **Enter**.

Opens apps FASTER than Launchpad or Dock!

Lazy Level: Open any app in 1 second—no clicking required!

Final Thoughts: Spotlight Search = Your Ultimate Productivity Tool!

Now you know how to:
Find files, emails, contacts, and messages instantly.
Do quick calculations, conversions, and definitions.
Open system settings and launch apps instantly.
Search the web and preview files without opening them.

Try ⌘ + Spacebar right now & search for something—you'll never go back!
Bonus Tips: Master Spotlight Search Like a Power User!

Now that you know **Spotlight can do way more than just find files**, here are some **extra pro tricks** to make it even more powerful!

---

1. Use Spotlight to Find Recently Opened Documents

Need to find a document you worked on recently? Spotlight can do it instantly!

How to do it:
· Type **"Documents opened last week"** → Shows all recent documents.
· Type **"edited:today"** → Lists all files modified today.

Now, no more hunting for recent work—it's all in one place!

Lazy Level: Find your latest work in seconds—no clicking required!

---

2. Search for Images, Music, and Videos Instantly

Spotlight can filter by file type so you can find media files FAST!

How to do it:
- kind:image → Shows all images on your Mac.
- kind:music → Lists all music files.
- kind:video → Instantly finds videos.

Perfect for finding old photos or videos hidden in your folders!

Lazy Level: Search only for the files you need—without Finder!

---

3. Use Spotlight to Check Stock Prices Instantly

No need to open a finance app—Spotlight shows stock updates instantly!

How to do it:
- AAPL stock → Shows Apple's stock price.
- TSLA stock → Instantly see Tesla's latest price.

Now you can track the market without opening a browser!

Lazy Level: Check stocks in 1 second—no app needed!

---

4. Open Websites Instantly Without Safari

Skip opening Safari—Spotlight can launch websites instantly!

How to do it:
• Type YouTube.com → Press **Enter** → Opens in Safari.
• Type Gmail → Spotlight suggests opening Gmail in the browser.

Now, you don't have to type full URLs in Safari—just use Spotlight!

Lazy Level: Launch your favorite sites in a single keystroke!

---

5. Find Apps Even If You Forget Their Names

Remember what the app does, but not its name? Spotlight can still find it!

How to do it:
• Type spreadsheet → Finds Excel, Numbers, or Google Sheets.
• Type photo editor → Suggests Photoshop, Pixelmator, or Preview.

No need to remember exact names—Spotlight understands descriptions!

Lazy Level: Your Mac just "knows" what you're looking for!

---

6. Search Within Specific Folders (Like Downloads or Documents)

Need to limit your search to a specific folder? Use this trick!

How to do it:
• folder:Downloads presentation → Finds "presentation" only in

Downloads.

• folder:Documents budget → Searches only inside Documents.

No more getting results from all over your Mac—just where you need!

Lazy Level: Laser-target your search results instantly!

---

7. Use Natural Language to Find Files & Emails

Spotlight understands natural language—just type like you talk!

How to do it:

• Emails from last week → Finds all emails from last week.
• Photos from last summer → Shows your summer vacation pictures.
• Documents I worked on in March → Lists files modified in March.

No need for complex search commands—just describe what you need!

Lazy Level: Search like a human, not a computer!

---

8. Move Files Instantly Without Finder

Found a file in Spotlight? Move it FAST!

How to do it:
1. Search for a file in Spotlight.
2. Drag it **directly from Spotlight to a folder or desktop!**

No need to open Finder—just drag & drop from Spotlight!

Lazy Level: Move files in seconds—without opening windows!

---

9. Use Spotlight to Instantly Convert Time Zones

Need to know what time it is in another country? Spotlight has you covered!

How to do it:
- time in Tokyo → Shows Tokyo's current time.
- New York to London time → Converts the time difference instantly.

Perfect for scheduling international meetings without a time zone calculator!

Lazy Level: No more Googling time zones—just type & get results!

---

10. Search for System Files & Hidden Settings

Want to tweak macOS settings? Spotlight can take you right there!

How to do it:
- Terminal → Opens Terminal instantly.
- Activity Monitor → See what's using your CPU.
- System Preferences → Jump to any system setting.

No more clicking through menus—just search & open!

Lazy Level: Find system tools instantly—like a Mac power user!

Final Thoughts: Spotlight = The Fastest Way to Find Anything on Your Mac!

Now you know how to:

Find apps, files, messages, and emails instantly.

Do calculations, conversions, stock checks, and weather updates.

Use natural language and Boolean operators for precise searches.

Move files, open websites, and even check time zones instantly.

Try ⌘ + Spacebar right now & search for something—you'll NEVER waste time again!

CHAPTER 12: AUTOMATE YOUR MAC WITH SHORTCUTS & APPLESCRIPT – GET MORE DONE WITH LESS EFFORT

Do you **repeat the same tasks** every day on your Mac?
Do you **wish your Mac could handle boring tasks automatically** while you focus on important work?

 With Shortcuts & AppleScript, your Mac can do the work FOR you!
You can **automate repetitive tasks, open multiple apps at once, organize files, send pre-written emails, and more**—all with a single click or voice command!

This chapter will teach you how to **create powerful automations** to save **time and effort** every day.

1. What Are Shortcuts & AppleScript?

Shortcuts & AppleScript are built-in automation tools that let your Mac perform tasks automatically.

Shortcuts App → A **drag-and-drop tool** that lets you create simple automations without coding.
AppleScript → A **script-based automation tool** that lets you control apps and system settings with custom code.

Think of Shortcuts as "easy automation" and AppleScript as "advanced automation" for power users!

Lazy Level: Your Mac does the work—you just click a button!

---

2. How to Use the Shortcuts App (No Coding Required!)

The Shortcuts app makes automation EASY—just drag, drop, and run!

How to Open Shortcuts:
1. Press ⌘ + Spacebar → Type **Shortcuts** → Press **Enter**.
2. Click "+" **(Create Shortcut)** to make a new automation.
3. Drag and drop actions to build your shortcut.

Now, let's create your first automation!

---

3. Create a Simple Shortcut to Open Your Work Apps in One Click

Instead of opening multiple apps manually, launch them ALL at once with a single click!

How to do it:

1. Open **Shortcuts** → Click "+" (**New Shortcut**).
2. Click **"Add Action"** → **Search "Open App"**.
3. Select multiple apps (e.g., **Safari, Mail, Slack, Notes**).
4. Click **Done** → Name it **"Start Work"**.
5. Run it by clicking the shortcut OR saying:
• "Hey Siri, start work!"

Now, every morning, your Mac opens everything you need instantly!

Lazy Level: One click = Your workday is ready!

---

4. Automate File Management with Shortcuts

Automatically move, rename, and sort files with Shortcuts!

Example: Automatically Move Screenshots to a Folder
1. Open **Shortcuts** → Click "+" (**New Shortcut**).
2. Click **"Add Action"** → Search **"Get Latest Screenshot"**.
3. Click **"Add Action"** → Search **"Move File"**.
4. Choose a folder (e.g., **Screenshots** in Documents).
5. Click **Done** → Now, whenever you take a screenshot, it gets sorted automatically!

Perfect for keeping your desktop clean!

Lazy Level: No more dragging files manually—your Mac organizes them for you!

---

5. Automate Email Responses with Shortcuts

Send pre-written email replies with one click!

How to do it:

1. Open **Shortcuts** → Click "+" **(New Shortcut)**.
2. Click **"Add Action"** → Search **"Send Email"**.
3. Enter recipient, subject, and pre-written message.
4. Click **Done** → Name it **"Quick Reply"**.
5. Run it when you need to send a fast email response!

Great for customer support, quick replies, or follow-ups!

Lazy Level: One click = Email sent instantly!

---

6. How to Use AppleScript for More Advanced Automation

AppleScript is for advanced automation—it can control apps, move files, and even click buttons!

How to Open AppleScript Editor:
1. Press ⌘ + Spacebar → Type **Script Editor** → Press **Enter**.
2. Click **File** → **New** to create a new script.

Now, let's create a basic AppleScript automation!

---

7. Automate App Launch with AppleScript

Want to open multiple apps automatically? AppleScript can do it!

Copy & paste this script into Script Editor:
```
tell application "Safari" to activate
tell application "Mail" to activate
tell application "Slack" to activate
tell application "Notes" to activate
```
1. Click **Run** → Your apps open instantly!
2. Click **File** → **Save As** → Save it as **"Start Work.scpt"**.
3. Now, just double-click this script to start your workday

instantly!

Perfect for launching work apps in one go!

Lazy Level: One click = Mac sets up your workspace!

---

8. Automate File Sorting with AppleScript

Want to automatically move PDFs to a folder? AppleScript can handle it!

Copy & paste this script into Script Editor:

```
tell application "Finder"
    move every file of folder "Macintosh HD:Users:YourUsername:Desktop" to folder "Macintosh HD:Users:YourUsername:Documents:PDFs"
end tell
```

1. Replace "YourUsername" with your actual Mac username.
2. Click **Run** → All PDFs on your desktop move to your Documents folder!
3. Save it as **"Sort PDFs.scpt"** and run it anytime.

Now, your Mac organizes files automatically!

Lazy Level: No more dragging files—your Mac sorts them for you!

---

9. Automate System Settings with AppleScript

Want to toggle Wi-Fi, Do Not Disturb, or Dark Mode with a script?

Example: Toggle Dark Mode Instantly

```
tell application "System Events"
```

```
tell appearance preferences
    set dark mode to not dark mode
end tell
end tell
```

Now, just run this script to toggle Dark Mode on/off instantly!

Lazy Level: No need to dig through settings—just click & switch!

---

10. Schedule Mac Automations with Automator & Calendar

Want your Mac to run automations at specific times?

How to do it:

1. Open **Automator** → Create a new **Calendar Alarm**.
2. Add a Shortcut or AppleScript.
3. Save it → Choose when it should run.

Now, your Mac can open apps, organize files, or clean up automatically at set times!

Lazy Level: Your Mac works on autopilot—zero effort needed!

Final Thoughts: Automate EVERYTHING & Save Time on Your Mac!

Now you know how to:

Use Shortcuts to automate daily tasks without coding.
Create AppleScripts for advanced automations.
Open multiple apps, sort files, and send emails automatically.
Schedule automations so your Mac does the work for you!

Try setting up ONE automation today—your future self will thank you!

Bonus Tips: Master Mac Automation Like a Pro!

You've learned **how to automate tasks with Shortcuts & AppleScript**, but here are **extra power-user tricks** to take your Mac automation game even further!

---

1. Add Your Shortcuts to the Menu Bar for One-Click Access

Want to run your automations instantly? Add them to your Mac's menu bar!

How to do it:
1. Open **Shortcuts** → Click the shortcut you created.
2. Click the **Info (i) button**.
3. Toggle ON **"Pin in Menu Bar."**
4. Now, click the **Shortcuts icon in the menu bar** to run it instantly!

Perfect for quick automation access—no need to open the Shortcuts app!

Lazy Level: Your shortcuts are now one click away!

---

2. Set Up a Keyboard Shortcut to Run Your Favorite Automations

Want to trigger a shortcut without clicking anything? Assign it a keyboard shortcut!

How to do it:
1. Open **Shortcuts** → Click on a shortcut.
2. Click the **Info (i) button** → Choose **"Add Keyboard Shortcut."**
3. Press the keys you want to use (e.g., ⌘ + Option + W).
4. Now, pressing that shortcut runs the automation instantly!

Great for opening work apps, organizing files, or switching settings FAST!

Lazy Level: Your Mac follows your commands with a single keystroke!

---

3. Run AppleScripts Automatically at Startup

Want an AppleScript to run every time you turn on your Mac? Automate it!

How to do it:
1. Save your AppleScript as an **app**:
· Open **Script Editor** → **File** → **Export**.
· Choose **"Application"** as the file format.
2. Open **System Settings** → **General** → **Login Items**.
3. Click "**+**" and select your AppleScript app.

Now, your script runs automatically when you log in!

Lazy Level: Mac automations run the moment you turn it on!

---

4. Use Automator to Create a "Cleanup" Button for Your Desktop

Is your desktop always cluttered? Create a one-click cleanup button!

How to do it:
1. Open **Automator** → **New Application**.
2. Add an action: **"Move Finder Items"**.
3. Set the destination folder (e.g., "Desktop Cleanup").
4. Save it as **"Clean Desktop.app"**.

Now, double-click this app, and your Mac cleans itself up!

Lazy Level: One click = Instantly clean desktop!

---

5. Use Siri to Run Shortcuts with Voice Commands

Want to run automations without touching your Mac? Just talk to Siri!

How to do it:
1. Open **Shortcuts** → Click a shortcut.
2. Click the **Info (i) button** → Toggle ON **"Use with Siri."**
3. Say:
- *"Hey Siri, start my work apps!"*
- *"Hey Siri, organize my files!"*

Now, you can run automations hands-free!

Lazy Level: Just talk—your Mac does the rest!

---

6. Automate Your Mac's Do Not Disturb Mode

Want your Mac to go into "focus mode" at work? Automate it!

How to do it:
1. Open **Shortcuts** → Click "+" **(New Shortcut).**
2. Click **"Add Action"** → Search **"Set Focus".**
3. Choose **"Do Not Disturb"** → Set for **2 hours.**
4. Click **Done** → Name it **"Focus Mode".**
5. Run it whenever you need distraction-free work!

No more manually enabling Do Not Disturb!

Lazy Level: Click once, and your Mac blocks all distractions!

7. Schedule Mac Automations with Calendar Alerts

Want to run automations at specific times? Use Calendar Alerts!

How to do it:
1. Open **Calendar** → Create a new event.
2. Click **"Alert"** → **Choose "Open File."**
3. Select a **Shortcut or AppleScript app.**

Now, your automation runs at a scheduled time!

Lazy Level: Your Mac follows a schedule—without reminders!

8. Automate Moving Downloaded Files to Specific Folders

Tired of organizing your Downloads folder? Automate it!

How to do it:
1. Open **Shortcuts** → Click **"+" (New Shortcut).**
2. Click **"Add Action"** → **Choose "Find Files."**
3. Set: **Look in "Downloads"** → **Filter by File Type (e.g., PDFs).**
4. Add **"Move Files"** → **Choose the destination folder (e.g., Documents).**
5. Click **Done** → Run it whenever you need!

Now, files go where they belong automatically!

Lazy Level: No more manually sorting downloads!

9. Auto-Rename Files in Bulk with AppleScript

Need to rename multiple files fast? Use AppleScript!

Copy & paste this into Script Editor:

```
tell application "Finder"
    set fileList to every file of folder "Macintosh HD:Users:YourUsername:Desktop"
    repeat with f in fileList
        set name of f to "Project_" & (get name of f)
    end repeat
end tell
```

This renames all files on your desktop with "Project_" at the beginning!

Lazy Level: Rename 100 files in seconds—without manual effort!

---

10. Use AppleScript to Instantly Empty the Trash

Too lazy to empty the Trash? Let AppleScript handle it!

Copy & paste this into Script Editor:

```
tell application "Finder"
    empty trash
end tell
```

Now, running this script clears your Trash instantly!

Lazy Level: No more dragging files—just click & delete!

Final Thoughts: Automate Everything & Work Less!

Now you know how to:
Add shortcuts to the menu bar & assign keyboard shortcuts.
Run AppleScripts at login & schedule automations with

Calendar.

Use Siri for hands-free automation.

Auto-move, rename, and sort files without effort.

Automate system settings like Do Not Disturb & Dark Mode.

Try automating ONE repetitive task today—you'll save HOURS in the long run!

CHAPTER 13: MASTERING AIRDROP & SHARING – INSTANTLY SEND FILES, PHOTOS & MORE

Do you still use **email or USB drives** to move files between devices?

Do you **text yourself photos** just to transfer them from iPhone to Mac?

With AirDrop, you can send files, photos, videos, links, and more—instantly, wirelessly, and effortlessly!

AirDrop lets you **share content between Apple devices in seconds**, without cables, third-party apps, or cloud storage.

In this chapter, you'll learn **how to master AirDrop, troubleshoot common issues, and unlock pro-sharing tricks** to transfer files faster than ever.

---

1. What is AirDrop & Why Should You Use It?

AirDrop is a built-in Apple feature that lets you wirelessly send files between Mac, iPhone, iPad, and even other people's devices.

Why it's amazing:
· **Works with all Apple devices** (Mac, iPhone, iPad).
· **Transfers files FAST** over Wi-Fi & Bluetooth.
· **No internet required**—works offline!
· **Send anything** (photos, videos, PDFs, contacts, links, and even entire folders).
· **Ultra-secure encryption** keeps your files private.

Think of AirDrop as the "teleportation" feature for files!

Lazy Level: No cables, no cloud, no hassle—just instant transfers!

---

2. How to Enable AirDrop on Mac & iPhone

Before using AirDrop, make sure it's enabled on both devices.

Step 1: Turn On AirDrop on Mac
1. Open **Finder** → Click **AirDrop (left sidebar).**
2. Click **"Allow me to be discovered by"** → **Choose one:**
· **Contacts Only** → Only people in your contacts can send you files.
· **Everyone** → Any nearby Apple device can send you files.

Pro Tip: If AirDrop isn't working, make sure **Wi-Fi & Bluetooth** are both ON.

Step 2: Turn On AirDrop on iPhone/iPad
1. Open **Control Center** (Swipe down from the top-right on Face

ID devices, or up from the bottom on Home button devices).

2. Press & hold the **Wi-Fi/Bluetooth tile** → Tap **AirDrop**.

3. Choose:

· **Contacts Only** → Recommended for privacy.

· **Everyone for 10 Minutes** → Best for quick sharing.

Now, your iPhone & Mac can send files to each other instantly!

---

3. How to AirDrop Files from Mac to iPhone & iPad

Transferring files between Mac & iPhone is as easy as drag & drop!

How to do it:

1. **Open Finder** on Mac → Click **AirDrop**.

2. **Drag any file** (photo, video, PDF, etc.) onto your iPhone's name.

3. Accept the file on your **iPhone** → **It's saved instantly!**

Perfect for moving documents, photos, or even entire folders FAST!

Lazy Level: No cables, no emails—just instant sharing!

---

4. How to AirDrop from iPhone to Mac

Sending files from iPhone to Mac is even easier!

How to do it:

1. **Select a file** (Photo, Note, Safari link, etc.).

2. Tap the **Share button** → Tap **AirDrop**.

3. Select your **Mac's name** → File appears on your Mac instantly!

Perfect for transferring photos, scanned PDFs, and copied text!

Lazy Level: No more emailing files to yourself—just AirDrop!

5. What Can You Send via AirDrop?

AirDrop isn't just for photos—you can share almost anything!

Things You Can AirDrop:
- **Photos & Videos** (Instantly send high-quality files—no compression!)
- **Documents & PDFs** (Move files between devices without USB drives)
- **Safari Links** (Instantly send a webpage from Mac to iPhone)
- **Music & Audio Files** (Move songs & recordings between devices)
- **Contacts** (Share phone numbers in seconds)
- **Map Locations** (Send pinned locations from Mac to iPhone Maps)
- **Clipboard Text** (Copy something on Mac → Paste it on iPhone instantly!)

Pro Tip: You can even AirDrop entire **folders** from Mac to iPhone/iPad!

Lazy Level: If it's on your screen, you can probably AirDrop it!

6. Troubleshooting AirDrop (Fix It When It's Not Working!)

Is AirDrop not showing up? Here's how to fix it!

Try These Fixes:
1. **Make sure Wi-Fi & Bluetooth are ON** (On both devices).
2. **Ensure "Allow AirDrop from Everyone" is enabled.**
3. **Move closer** (AirDrop works best within 30 feet).

4. **Restart both devices** (90% of AirDrop problems are fixed with a restart).

5. **Disable AirDrop Restrictions**:

· Go to **Settings** → **Screen Time** → **Content & Privacy Restrictions** → **Allowed Apps** → Make sure **AirDrop** is ON.

Now, AirDrop should work instantly again!

Lazy Level: Troubleshooting takes 30 seconds—problem solved!

---

7. Pro AirDrop Tricks to Transfer Even Faster

1. AirDrop Multiple Files at Once (Batch Transfer)

Sending more than one file? Do it in one tap!

How to do it:
· Select **multiple photos or files** → Tap **Share** → **AirDrop** → Select Mac/iPhone.
Saves time when moving large batches of files!

Lazy Level: Why send one at a time? Batch-transfer EVERYTHING!

---

2. AirDrop Clipboard Text from Mac to iPhone

Copy text on your Mac → **Paste it on iPhone without typing!**

How to do it:
1. Copy text on Mac (⌘ + C).
2. Open iPhone → **Long-press in any text field** → **Paste**.

Perfect for sharing passwords, links, or notes FAST!

Lazy Level: No email, no messaging—just copy & paste across devices!

---

3. AirDrop Safari Tabs Between Devices

Reading something on Mac? Send the tab to iPhone instantly!

How to do it:
1. Open **Safari** on Mac → Click **Share** → **AirDrop**.
2. Select your **iPhone** → The webpage opens instantly!

No need to retype URLs—just AirDrop the tab!

Lazy Level: Move between Mac & iPhone browsing seamlessly!

---

4. Use AirDrop to Share Wi-Fi Passwords Instantly

Need to share your Wi-Fi with a friend? AirDrop does it instantly!

How to do it:
1. Make sure both devices have **Wi-Fi & Bluetooth ON**.
2. When their iPhone tries to connect to your Wi-Fi, you'll get a **"Share Password"** prompt.
3. Tap **"Share Password"** → They're instantly connected!

No need to type long Wi-Fi passwords ever again!

Lazy Level: One tap = Instant Wi-Fi access for guests!

Final Thoughts: Master AirDrop & Never Struggle with File Transfers Again!

Now you know how to:

Enable AirDrop & transfer files between Mac, iPhone, & iPad.
Send photos, documents, links, and clipboard text instantly.
Fix AirDrop when it's not working.
Use pro tricks like batch transfers, Safari tab sharing, & Wi-Fi password sharing.

Try AirDropping a file from Mac to iPhone NOW—you'll never go back to emailing yourself again!
Bonus Tips: Take AirDrop & Sharing to the Next Level!

You already know **how to send files between Mac, iPhone, and iPad instantly**, but here are **pro-level AirDrop tricks** to make sharing even FASTER and more powerful!

---

1. AirDrop Entire Folders (Skip Zipping & Unzipping!)

Did you know you can AirDrop full folders from Mac to iPhone/iPad?

How to do it:
1. Open **Finder** on Mac.
2. **Right-click any folder** → Click **Share** → **AirDrop**.
3. Select your **iPhone or iPad** → Accept the transfer.

Perfect for transferring work projects, photo albums, or large collections of files in one step!

Lazy Level: Skip file compression—just AirDrop whole folders!

---

2. AirDrop Links Between Devices Without Copy-Paste

Don't copy-paste a URL manually—just AirDrop it!

How to do it:
1. Open **Safari (or any browser)** on Mac or iPhone.
2. Tap the **Share button → AirDrop**.
3. Select your other device → The link opens instantly!

Works for YouTube videos, Google Docs, or any website!

Lazy Level: No need to type long URLs—just AirDrop & go!

---

3. Transfer Passwords Securely with AirDrop

Sharing a password with a trusted friend or colleague? Send it securely!

How to do it:
1. Open **Settings → Passwords** on iPhone.
2. Select a saved password → Tap **Share → AirDrop**.
3. Choose the recipient's **iPhone/Mac** → They receive the login details securely.

No need for texts or screenshots—AirDrop keeps it private!

Lazy Level: One tap = Secure password sharing!

---

4. Use AirDrop to Instantly Move Voice Memos to Mac

Recorded a voice memo on iPhone? Move it to Mac instantly!

How to do it:
1. Open **Voice Memos** on iPhone.
2. Select a recording → Tap **Share → AirDrop**.

3. Choose your **Mac** → File transfers instantly.

Now, you can edit or transcribe voice notes on Mac with no extra steps!

Lazy Level: Move audio files instantly—no emailing required!

---

5. AirDrop Files Directly to Apps (Skip Finder & Downloads!)

Did you know you can send files directly into an app, skipping Finder?

How to do it:
1. AirDrop a file from **iPhone to Mac**.
2. Instead of saving it to Finder, **choose an app** (e.g., Photos, Keynote, Notes).

Perfect for sending images directly into Photoshop or PDFs straight into Preview!

Lazy Level: No need to move files manually—AirDrop sends them where you need!

---

6. Change Your AirDrop Name for Faster Transfers

If you have multiple Apple devices, rename them to avoid confusion!

How to do it:
1. On Mac: **System Settings** → **General** → **About** → **Name**.
2. On iPhone: **Settings** → **General** → **About** → **Name**.

Now, no more guessing which "John's iPhone" to send files to!

Lazy Level: Easier & faster file transfers—no mix-ups!

---

7. Use AirDrop to Share Apple Notes Instantly

Need to share a to-do list or meeting notes? AirDrop it!

How to do it:
1. Open **Notes** on Mac or iPhone.
2. Tap the **Share button** → **AirDrop**.
3. Choose your **Mac or iPhone** → Note appears instantly!

Perfect for sharing quick reminders, work notes, or shopping lists!

Lazy Level: Forget copy-paste—AirDrop Notes in seconds!

---

8. Quickly Fix "No People Found" in AirDrop

Can't find someone nearby in AirDrop? Try this fix!

How to do it:
1. **Make sure both devices have Wi-Fi & Bluetooth ON.**
2. **Turn AirDrop OFF & ON** (Go to Control Center → Tap AirDrop → Toggle OFF & ON).
3. **Bring devices closer together** (AirDrop works best within 30 feet).
4. **Try switching AirDrop to "Everyone for 10 Minutes."**

Works 99% of the time when AirDrop isn't detecting devices!

Lazy Level: Fix AirDrop in 5 seconds—no frustration!

---

9. Set Up AirDrop on Mac's Dock for Even Faster Sharing

Want to AirDrop files even faster? Add it to your Dock!

How to do it:
1. Open **Finder** → Drag **AirDrop (left sidebar) to the Dock.**
2. Now, just **drag files onto the Dock icon** to send them via AirDrop!

No need to open Finder—just drag & drop to share instantly!

Lazy Level: Cut AirDrop time in half—just drop files on the Dock!

---

10. AirDrop from iPhone to Mac Even When They Use Different Apple IDs

Need to send a file to a Mac that's not signed into your iCloud?

How to do it:
1. Set AirDrop on Mac to **"Everyone for 10 Minutes."**
2. Send the file from iPhone → Accept the transfer on Mac.

Now, you can share files between work and personal devices easily!

Lazy Level: No need to log into the same Apple ID—just AirDrop it!

Final Thoughts: AirDrop = The Ultimate File Sharing Hack!

Now you know how to:
AirDrop folders, clipboard text, passwords, and Safari links.
Send files directly to apps without saving to Finder.
Rename devices for faster transfers & fix common AirDrop

issues.

Use AirDrop in the Dock for even quicker file sharing.

Try AirDropping something RIGHT NOW—it's a game-changer!

CHAPTER 14: MASTERING MULTIPLE DESKTOPS & MISSION CONTROL – NAVIGATE YOUR MAC LIKE A PRO

Do you **struggle with too many open windows** cluttering your Mac?

Do you **lose track of apps and files** while multitasking?

 With Multiple Desktops & Mission Control, you can keep everything organized, switch between tasks instantly, and boost your productivity!

No more window chaos—just **smooth navigation and efficient workflows** across your Mac.

In this chapter, you'll learn how to **master Multiple Desktops, Mission Control, and advanced window management tricks** to work smarter, not harder.

---

1. What Are Multiple Desktops & Mission Control?

 Mission Control is a macOS feature that lets you manage all your open windows, apps, and Desktops with a single view.

Multiple Desktops (also called Spaces) allow you to create separate workspaces, so you can organize your workflow better.

Why they're amazing:

• **Declutter your screen** by organizing different tasks on different Desktops.

• **Switch between tasks instantly** without minimizing or closing apps.

• **Keep work & personal apps separate** (e.g., Work Desktop & Entertainment Desktop).

• **Use full-screen apps efficiently** (each app gets its own Desktop).

Think of Mission Control as a "command center" for all your windows!

Lazy Level: No more window chaos—just smooth, organized multitasking!

---

2. How to Open Mission Control & View Multiple Desktops

Mission Control gives you a bird's-eye view of all open windows & Desktops.

Ways to Open Mission Control:

1. **Swipe up with three fingers** on the trackpad (FASTEST way).

2. **Press F3 (Mission Control key)** or Control + ↑ (Up Arrow).

3. **Use Hot Corners:**

• Go to **System Settings → Desktop & Dock → Mission Control → Hot Corners**.

• Set a corner to **"Mission Control"**, so moving your mouse there activates it.

Now, you can instantly see ALL open windows & Desktops!

Lazy Level: One swipe = Total control over your Mac!

---

3. How to Create & Use Multiple Desktops (Spaces)

Multiple Desktops let you separate different tasks for better organization.

How to Create a New Desktop:
1. Open **Mission Control (F3 or Swipe Up with Three Fingers)**.
2. Click the **"+" button in the top-right corner**.
3. A new Desktop appears—switch between them by **swiping left or right with three fingers**.

Now, you can have separate Desktops for different tasks!

Lazy Level: One swipe = Instant workspace switch!

---

4. Best Ways to Use Multiple Desktops for Maximum Productivity

Want to work smarter? Organize your Desktops like this!

1. Create a Desktop for Each Task or Project
- **Desktop 1:** Work apps (Safari, Word, Slack).
- **Desktop 2:** Creative apps (Photoshop, Final Cut Pro).
- **Desktop 3:** Entertainment (Spotify, YouTube, Netflix).

Keeps your workflow organized & distraction-free!

---

2. Use Full-Screen Apps on Their Own Desktops

Full-screen apps automatically get their own Desktop—use them wisely!

How to do it:

1. Click the **green "maximize" button** in the top-left of any app.
2. The app moves to its own Desktop.
3. Swipe between full-screen apps with **three-finger swipes**.

Perfect for focused work without distractions!

---

3. Assign Apps to Specific Desktops (So They Always Open in the Right Place!)

Keep apps organized by assigning them to fixed Desktops!

How to do it:

1. Open an app → Right-click its icon in the Dock.
2. Go to **Options → Assign To → This Desktop**.
3. Now, that app will always open on the same Desktop!

Great for keeping Mail on Desktop 1, Photoshop on Desktop 2, etc.

Lazy Level: Apps open where you want—no dragging required!

---

4. Use Hotkeys to Switch Desktops Faster

Want to switch Desktops instantly? Use these shortcuts!

Best Keyboard Shortcuts for Multiple Desktops:
• Control + Left/Right Arrow → Switch Desktops FAST!
• Control + Number (1, 2, 3...) → Jump directly to a specific

Desktop.

No more swiping—just jump to the right Desktop in seconds!

Lazy Level: Keyboard shortcuts = Instant workspace changes!

---

5. Master Window Snapping & Split View for Ultimate Efficiency

macOS has built-in window snapping & Split View for better multitasking!

How to Use Split View (Two Apps Side-by-Side):
1. Click & hold the **green maximize button** on any window.
2. Drag it to the **left or right**.
3. Choose another app to fill the other half of the screen.

Now, you can work on two apps side by side!

Lazy Level: No more switching windows—work on two apps at once!

---

6. Use Stage Manager for Even More Organized Multitasking

Stage Manager (macOS Ventura & later) helps organize open apps automatically!

How to enable it:
1. Open **System Settings** → **Desktop & Dock**.
2. Turn ON **Stage Manager**.
3. Now, your open apps are neatly grouped on the side for easy switching.

Perfect for managing multiple projects at once!

Lazy Level: No more window clutter—just focus & work efficiently!

---

7. Bonus Tricks for Mastering Multiple Desktops & Mission Control

1. Quickly Move Windows Between Desktops

Want to move an app to another Desktop? Just drag it!

How to do it:
1. Open **Mission Control.**
2. Drag a window from one Desktop to another.

Now, you can instantly reorganize your workspaces!

---

2. Use Mission Control with External Displays

Multiple monitors? Each one can have its own set of Desktops!

How to do it:
· **Go to System Settings** → **Displays** → Enable **"Displays have separate Spaces."**
· Now, each screen can have its own **Mission Control & Desktops!**

Perfect for dual-monitor setups & better multitasking!

---

3. Close Desktops to Declutter Your Workspace

Too many Desktops? Delete them in seconds!

How to do it:
1. Open **Mission Control.**

2. Hover over a Desktop → Click the **"X" button** in the top-left.

Now, you keep only the Desktops you need!

Lazy Level: No more clutter—just smooth workflow management!

Final Thoughts: Master Multiple Desktops & Mission Control for Peak Productivity!

Now you know how to:

Use Mission Control to organize windows like a pro.

Create Multiple Desktops for different tasks & workflows.

Assign apps to Desktops & switch between them instantly.

Use Split View, window snapping, & Stage Manager for better multitasking.

Try setting up at least TWO Desktops right now—you'll never go back!

Bonus Tips: Master Multiple Desktops & Mission Control Like a Pro!

Now that you know **how to organize your Mac with Multiple Desktops & Mission Control**, here are **power-user tricks** to make it even **faster, smoother, and more efficient!**

---

1. Instantly Move a Window to Another Desktop (Without Mission Control!)

Dragging windows in Mission Control is slow—use this shortcut instead!

How to do it:

1. Click & hold the **window's title bar**.

2. Press Control + Number Key (1, 2, 3...) to instantly move it to that Desktop.

No need to open Mission Control—just send apps where they belong in one step!

Lazy Level: Move windows in seconds—no dragging required!

---

2. Assign Different Wallpapers to Each Desktop for Visual Separation

Easily distinguish your Desktops by setting different wallpapers!

How to do it:
1. Switch to a Desktop (Control + Left/Right Arrow).
2. Open **System Settings → Wallpaper**.
3. Choose a **unique wallpaper** for each Desktop.

Now, you'll instantly know which Desktop you're on—no confusion!

Lazy Level: Separate work & play visually!

---

3. Auto-Switch Desktops When Opening Specific Apps

Want Mail to always open on Desktop 1 and Photoshop on Desktop 2? Automate it!

How to do it:
1. Open the app.
2. Right-click its icon in the Dock → Click **Options → Assign To → This Desktop**.
3. Repeat for other apps to keep them in their assigned spaces.

Now, your Mac keeps everything organized automatically!

Lazy Level: Apps go where they belong—without manual dragging!

---

4. Set Up "Work Mode" and "Relax Mode" Desktops for Instant Productivity

Want a distraction-free work environment? Set up separate modes!

Example Desktop Setup:
· **Desktop 1 = Work Apps** (Slack, Chrome, Notes, Excel)
· **Desktop 2 = Research & Writing** (Safari, Word)
· **Desktop 3 = Entertainment & Breaks** (Spotify, YouTube)

Now, you can "enter work mode" or "relax mode" in one swipe!

Lazy Level: No distractions—just smooth workflow switching!

---

5. Use Stage Manager & Mission Control Together for Maximum Efficiency

Mission Control + Stage Manager = Ultimate window management!

How to do it:
1. Enable **Stage Manager (System Settings → Desktop & Dock → Stage Manager ON)**.
2. Swipe into **Mission Control (F3 or Three-Finger Swipe Up)** to see all your open Desktops.
3. Switch Desktops & quickly bring up the app group you need.

Perfect for keeping multiple projects organized!

Lazy Level: All your apps, files, and workspaces are perfectly sorted!

---

6. Use Hot Corners to Activate Mission Control Instantly

Want to access Mission Control even faster? Just move your mouse!

How to do it:
1. Open **System Settings → Desktop & Dock → Mission Control → Hot Corners.**
2. Set **a corner to "Mission Control".**
3. Now, move your mouse to that corner → Mission Control opens instantly!

No keyboard shortcuts needed—just move your mouse!

Lazy Level: Instant window & Desktop management—effortless!

---

7. Lock Desktops to Prevent Accidental Window Switching

Accidentally switching Desktops while scrolling? Lock them in place!

How to do it:
1. Go to **System Settings → Accessibility → Pointer Control.**
2. Turn ON **"Disable Trackpad Gesture for Switching Spaces."**

Now, swiping left/right won't accidentally move your windows!

Lazy Level: No more unintentional Desktop switching!

8. Snap Windows to Specific Desktop Positions for Better Organization

Keep frequently used windows in the same position on every Desktop!

How to do it:
1. Open an app on **Desktop 1**.
2. Drag it to a **specific position** (e.g., Notes on the left, Safari on the right).
3. Repeat for each Desktop, keeping apps in the same spots.

Now, switching Desktops feels consistent & seamless!

Lazy Level: Same layout on every Desktop = Instant muscle memory!

9. Instantly Close Extra Desktops When You No Longer Need Them

Too many Desktops? Clean up in seconds!

How to do it:
1. Open **Mission Control (F3 or Three-Finger Swipe Up)**.
2. Hover over a Desktop's thumbnail → Click the **"X" button**.

Declutter your workspaces instantly!

Lazy Level: Less mess, more productivity!

10. Set Up a "Presentation Desktop" for Screen Sharing & Video

Calls

Need a clean, distraction-free Desktop for Zoom calls or presentations?

How to do it:
1. Create a new Desktop (F3 → + button).
2. Open ONLY the apps needed for the call (e.g., Zoom, Keynote).
3. Keep your main Desktop messy—no one will see it!

Now, your screen looks professional, even if your real workspace is chaos!

Lazy Level: Appear ultra-organized in video calls—without cleaning up!

Final Thoughts: Master Multiple Desktops & Mission Control for Peak Productivity!

Now you know how to:

Use hotkeys, Hot Corners, & swipes for faster Desktop switching.

Keep different Desktops for work, creative tasks, and entertainment.

Lock Desktops, snap windows, and organize apps for seamless navigation.

Set up a distraction-free Desktop for work, meetings, and presentations.

Try setting up 3 Desktops NOW—you'll never go back to messy windows again!

Bonus Tips: Become a Finder Power User & Manage Files Like a Pro!

You've already learned how to **navigate, search, and organize files efficiently** with Finder. Now, let's take it even further with **expert-level tricks** that will make file management effortless!

---

1. Pin Your Most-Used Folders to the Sidebar for Instant Access

Tired of searching for the same folders over and over? Pin them for quick access!

How to do it:

1. Open Finder → Locate your most-used folder.
2. Drag it to the **Sidebar** under "Favorites."
3. Now, it's always available in one click!

Perfect for instant access to work files, projects, or downloads!

Lazy Level: No more digging through folders—just one-click access!

---

2. Create an "Inbox" Folder for Quick File Sorting

Need a temporary place to store files before organizing them? Create an "Inbox" folder!

How to do it:

1. Open Finder → Create a new folder called **Inbox**.
2. Drag all random downloads, screenshots, and temporary files here.
3. Sort them later when you have time!

Keeps your Desktop & Downloads folder clutter-free!

Lazy Level: Dump first, organize later—zero stress!

3. Use Finder's "Recents" Folder to Instantly Find Recent Files

Need to find a file you just worked on? Don't search manually —use Recents!

How to do it:
1. Open Finder → Click **Recents (Sidebar).**
2. This shows all **recently opened, modified, or created files.**

No need to remember where you saved it—Finder remembers for you!

Lazy Level: Instant file recovery—no searching needed!

4. Copy a File's Full Path for Quick Sharing

Need to tell someone exactly where a file is located? Copy its full path!

How to do it:
1. Right-click the file → Click **Get Info.**
2. Find the **"Where"** section → Copy the file path.
3. OR **Press Option + Right-click on the file** → Choose "Copy [File] as Pathname".

Perfect for sending file locations in emails or messages!

Lazy Level: No more "Where is that file?" moments!

5. Move Files Instantly with a Keyboard Shortcut (No Dragging!)

Instead of dragging files, move them instantly with a shortcut!

How to do it:

1. Select a file in Finder.
2. Press ⌘ + C to copy.
3. Navigate to the destination folder.
4. Press ⌘ + Option + V → The file **moves** instead of copying!

Now, you can move files without opening multiple Finder windows!

Lazy Level: Less clicking, more doing!

---

6. Open Finder Faster by Setting It as Your Default New Window

Want Finder to always open in your favorite folder? Customize it!

How to do it:

1. Open Finder → Click **Finder** → **Settings** → **General**.
2. Under **"New Finder windows show"**, select your preferred default folder (e.g., **Documents, Downloads, or Work Folder**).

Now, every new Finder window opens exactly where you want!

Lazy Level: No more navigating—just open & go!

---

7. Quickly Show or Hide Hidden Files

Mac hides system files by default, but you can toggle them on/

off instantly!

How to do it:
• **Press ⌘ + Shift + . (period)** → Hidden files appear/disappear.

Perfect for accessing system files or troubleshooting!

Lazy Level: See everything with a single shortcut!

---

8. Rename Multiple Files at Once (Batch Renaming!)

Need to rename 100 files? Don't do it manually!

How to do it:
1. Select multiple files → Right-click → **Rename**.
2. Choose from:
• **Replace Text** → Change part of the name (e.g., rename "IMG_001" to "Vacation_001").
• **Add Text** → Add a prefix or suffix (e.g., "Project_Files_01").
• **Format Names** → Number them automatically (e.g., "Report_1, Report_2, Report_3").

Now, renaming large batches of files takes seconds!

Lazy Level: Rename hundreds of files in one step!

---

9. Auto-Sort Files by Type, Date, or Tags for Instant Organization

Manually sorting files is a waste of time—let Finder do it for you!

How to do it:
• Open Finder → Click **View** → **Sort By**.

- Choose **Name, Date Modified, File Type, or Tags**.
- For auto-grouping, click **View → Use Groups** to separate files neatly.

Finder automatically organizes your files every time you open a folder!

Lazy Level: Your files stay sorted—without effort!

---

10. Use Quick Actions for Instant File Edits (Without Opening Apps!)

Need to rotate an image, sign a PDF, or trim a video? Do it directly in Finder!

How to do it:
1. Select a file → Click **the Quick Actions button (bottom-right of Finder window)**.
2. Choose from options like **Rotate, Convert to PDF, Trim Video, Markup, or Add Signature**.

Now, you can edit files instantly—without opening any apps!

Lazy Level: Quick edits, no extra steps!

Final Thoughts: Finder = The Ultimate Mac File Manager!

Now you know how to:
Navigate Finder faster with shortcuts & pinned folders.
Use Tags, Smart Folders, and Auto-Sorting for effortless file organization.
Batch rename, move, and edit files in seconds.
Use Quick Look, Quick Actions, and Smart Search to work faster.

Try using ⌘ + Space or Finder's search bar RIGHT NOW— you'll never struggle to find a file again!

CHAPTER 15: MAC MAINTENANCE & PERFORMANCE HACKS – KEEP YOUR MAC RUNNING FAST & SMOOTH

Is your **Mac running slow?**

Do you experience **spinning beach balls, laggy performance, or battery drain?**

 With the right maintenance tricks, your Mac can stay as fast as new—even after years of use!

Most people never optimize their Mac, but with a few simple steps, you can **boost speed, free up storage, and improve battery life.**

In this final chapter, you'll learn **the best Mac maintenance and performance hacks** to keep your system running smoothly—without needing third-party tools or constant troubleshooting.

---

1. Restart Your Mac Regularly (The Simplest Performance

Boost!)

Leaving your Mac on for weeks? Restarting it clears memory, refreshes system processes, and improves performance.

How to do it:
• Click **Apple Menu → Restart.**
• Restart **at least once a week** (or daily if you use heavy apps like Photoshop or Final Cut Pro).

Your Mac will feel instantly faster—no effort needed!

Lazy Level: A 1-minute restart = Instant performance boost!

---

2. Free Up RAM & Close Unnecessary Apps

Too many open apps can slow down your Mac. Close what you don't need!

How to check RAM usage:
1. Open **Activity Monitor (⌘ + Space → Type "Activity Monitor").**
2. Click the **Memory tab** → Look for apps using high memory (marked in red or yellow).
3. Select them → Click **"X" (Force Quit).**

Your Mac will run much smoother when unnecessary apps aren't hogging RAM!

Lazy Level: Close unused apps & free up memory instantly!

---

3. Remove Startup Apps to Speed Up Boot Time

Too many startup apps = Slow Mac startup! Disable the ones

you don't need.

How to do it:
1. Go to **System Settings** → **General** → **Login Items**.
2. Look for unnecessary apps → Click "-" **to remove them.**

Now, your Mac will start up MUCH faster!

Lazy Level: Less waiting, more doing!

---

4. Keep Your Storage Clean (Macs Slow Down When Nearly Full!)

A nearly full hard drive can slow down your Mac—free up space regularly!

How to check your storage:
1. Click ☐ **Apple Menu** → **About This Mac** → **Storage**.
2. If you have less than **10GB free**, it's time to clean up!

How to free up space fast:
· Delete **large, old files** (⌘ + Space → Type "Large Files" → Delete Unused Ones).
· Empty **Trash** (Right-click Trash → Empty Trash).
· Remove **duplicate files** using Finder search (kind:document name:copy).
· Store files in **iCloud or an external drive**.

Your Mac will run MUCH faster with at least 20% free space!

Lazy Level: A clean Mac = A fast Mac!

---

5. Clear Cache & Temporary Files for a Speed Boost

macOS stores temporary cache files that take up space & slow things down over time.

How to delete cache manually:
1. Open Finder → Click **Go** → **Go to Folder**.
2. Type: ~/Library/Caches/ → Press **Enter**.
3. Delete everything inside (Don't worry—macOS recreates necessary files).

Now, your Mac will feel snappier & have more free space!

Lazy Level: Delete junk files = Instant performance boost!

---

6. Update macOS & Apps for Maximum Efficiency

Keeping macOS and apps updated improves speed, security, and battery life!

How to do it:
1. Go to **System Settings** → **General** → **Software Update**.
2. Click **"Update Now"** if an update is available.
3. Open the **App Store** → **Click Updates** → Update all apps.

Updates fix bugs, speed up performance & add new features!

Lazy Level: Set auto-updates & never worry about it again!

---

7. Use Disk Utility to Fix Errors & Optimize Your Mac

Your Mac's hard drive can develop small errors over time—Disk Utility fixes them!

How to do it:

1. Open **Disk Utility** (⌘ + **Space** → **Type "Disk Utility"**).
2. Select **Macintosh HD** → Click **First Aid** → Run.

Fixes file system errors & improves speed automatically!

Lazy Level: Click a button → Your Mac fixes itself!

---

8. Use Activity Monitor to Find & Kill CPU-Hogging Apps

Some apps secretly use too much processing power, slowing everything down!

How to check CPU usage:
1. Open **Activity Monitor** (⌘ + **Space** → **Type "Activity Monitor"**).
2. Click the **CPU tab** → Look for apps using 80% or more CPU.
3. Select the app → Click **"X" (Force Quit).**

Your Mac will feel smoother instantly after quitting resource-hogging apps!

Lazy Level: One click = Instant speed boost!

---

9. Reset PRAM & SMC for Hardware-Related Issues

If your Mac is overheating, acting weird, or crashing, resetting PRAM & SMC can fix it!

How to Reset PRAM (For Performance Issues):
1. Restart Mac → Hold Option + Command + P + R until the Apple logo appears.

How to Reset SMC (For Fan, Battery, or Power Issues):
• On **Intel Macs:**

1. Shut down Mac → Hold **Shift + Control + Option + Power button** for 10 sec.

2. Release & restart.

• On **Apple Silicon Macs**: Simply restart—SMC resets automatically!

Fixes weird bugs, overheating, & slow performance!

Lazy Level: Like a factory reset—but easier!

---

10. Extend Battery Life with These Power-Saving Tips

Want your Mac's battery to last longer? Try these simple tricks!

Best Battery-Saving Settings:

• **Lower screen brightness** (F1 key).

• **Turn off Bluetooth & Wi-Fi** when not needed.

• **Close background apps** (⌘ + Q for unused apps).

• **Use Safari instead of Chrome** (Chrome drains battery faster).

• **Enable Energy Saver Mode** (System Settings → Battery → Low Power Mode).

Your Mac will last HOURS longer on a single charge!

Lazy Level: More battery = More productivity!

Final Thoughts: Keep Your Mac Fast, Clean & Efficient Forever!

Now you know how to:

Restart, clear RAM, and remove startup apps for speed.

Free up storage, delete cache, and use Disk Utility to fix errors.

Monitor CPU-heavy apps & reset PRAM/SMC to fix common issues.

Improve battery life & keep your Mac running like new.

Try at least ONE of these tips NOW—your Mac will thank you! Bonus Tips: Keep Your Mac Running Like a Speed Demon!

You've already learned **the best ways to speed up, clean, and optimize your Mac**, but here are **extra power-user tricks** to take it even further!

---

1. Enable Reduce Motion & Transparency for Extra Speed

Animations and visual effects slow down older Macs—turn them off for a performance boost!

How to do it:
1. Open **System Settings → Accessibility → Display**.
2. Enable **Reduce Motion** and **Reduce Transparency**.

Now, macOS will feel snappier—especially on older devices!

Lazy Level: Less eye candy = More speed!

---

2. Find & Delete Large Unused Files Instantly

Got random huge files eating up storage? Find them FAST!

How to do it:
1. Open Finder → Press ⌘ + Space → Type **"Large Files"**.
2. Sort results by size → Delete files you don't need.

Now, you can free up 10GB+ in minutes!

Lazy Level: Less junk = More storage & speed!

---

3. Use Safari Instead of Chrome (Mac's Secret Performance Boost!)

Chrome is a RAM-hogging battery killer—Safari runs way better on macOS!

Why switch to Safari?
- Uses **less RAM & CPU** than Chrome.
- Saves **HOURS of battery life.**
- Syncs **better with Apple devices.**

Your Mac will run smoother & your battery will last longer!

Lazy Level: Ditch Chrome = Instant speed & battery boost!

---

4. Keep Your Desktop Clean (Yes, It Actually Speeds Up Your Mac!)

Every icon on your Desktop uses RAM—keep it minimal!

How to do it:
1. Move files into **folders** or use **Desktop Stacks** (Right-click Desktop → Use Stacks).
2. Keep no more than **5-10 files** on the Desktop.

Your Mac will boot & run faster instantly!

Lazy Level: A clean Desktop = A fast Mac!

---

5. Use Terminal to Purge RAM for Instant Performance Boost

Want a quick way to free up memory without restarting? Use this Terminal trick!

How to do it:

1. Open **Terminal (⌘ + Space → Type "Terminal")**.

2. Type:

sudo purge

3. Press **Enter**, enter your password, and watch your RAM get cleared instantly!

Perfect when your Mac starts slowing down after long usage!

Lazy Level: One command = Instant memory refresh!

---

6. Disable Unnecessary Extensions & Plugins

Extensions slow down browsers & apps—disable the ones you don't use!

How to do it:

1. **For Safari:** Open **Safari → Settings → Extensions** → Disable extras.

2. **For Chrome:** Open **Chrome → Extensions (chrome://extensions/)** → Remove unused ones.

Now, your browser will run much faster!

Lazy Level: Less bloat = Faster browsing!

---

7. Enable Auto-Empty Trash (So You Never Forget!)

Why manually empty the Trash? Let macOS do it for you!

How to do it:

1. Open **Finder → Settings → Advanced**.

2. Check **"Remove items from the Trash after 30 days."**

Now, your Trash never fills up & you always have free space!

Lazy Level: Trash empties itself—no effort required!

---

8. Schedule Automatic Restarts for Peak Performance

Restarting once a week keeps your Mac fast—schedule it automatically!

How to do it:
1. Open **System Settings → Battery → Schedule**.
2. Set **a weekly restart (e.g., Sunday at 3 AM).**

Your Mac will refresh itself while you sleep!

Lazy Level: Automatic restarts = No lag!

---

9. Use Activity Monitor's Energy Tab to Extend Battery Life

Want to know which apps are draining your battery? Find out in seconds!

How to do it:
1. Open **Activity Monitor (⌘ + Space → Type "Activity Monitor").**
2. Click the **Energy tab** → Look for apps with high energy impact.
3. Close apps that are killing your battery.

Your Mac's battery will last MUCH longer now!

Lazy Level: Less battery drain = More work time!

10. Enable Low Power Mode for Maximum Battery Life

Need your battery to last as long as possible? Enable Low Power Mode!

How to do it:

1. Open **System Settings → Battery**.
2. Turn ON **Low Power Mode** (works on both battery & plugged-in modes!).

Extends battery life by reducing background processes & screen brightness!

Lazy Level: More battery = More productivity!

Final Thoughts: Keep Your Mac Running Smooth & Fast Forever!

Now you know how to:

Purge RAM, free up storage, and clear caches.

Disable unnecessary startup apps, extensions, and animations.

Use Activity Monitor to kill CPU-hogging apps.

Optimize battery life with Low Power Mode & Energy Monitor.

Try at least ONE of these tips RIGHT NOW—your Mac will feel brand new!

Conclusion: Take Action & Make Your Mac Work for You!

Congratulations! You've made it to the end of this book, and by now, you've unlocked **powerful tricks, time-saving shortcuts, and hidden Mac features** that most users never discover.

But here's the secret: **Knowledge is only useful if you apply it.**

You now have **a complete toolbox** of productivity hacks—from mastering Finder, AirDrop, and Spotlight to automating tasks and optimizing performance. But these tips will only transform your experience if you **start using them today**.

What to Do Next? Start Small & Build Momentum!

You don't need to remember every trick right now. Instead, do this:
Pick 3 hacks from this book and start using them today.
Bookmark your favorite chapters so you can revisit them when needed.
Practice using shortcuts and automation to see how much time you save.

The more you use these tricks, the faster, smarter, and more effortlessly you'll use your Mac!

Enjoyed This Book? Your Review Matters!

If this book helped you **save time, boost productivity, or simply enjoy your Mac more**, I'd truly appreciate it if you could take a **minute to leave a positive review**.

Why Your Review Helps:
· It helps **other Mac users** discover these tricks.
· It motivates me to create **even more helpful content**.
· It lets me know which tips were most valuable for you!

If you found this book useful, please leave a ★★★★★**5-STAR REVIEW. It makes a huge difference!**

Keep Exploring & Keep Learning!

Your Mac is an incredibly powerful tool—**and now, you have the skills to make the most of it**.

Keep experimenting, keep optimizing, and most importantly—**keep having fun with your Mac!**

Thank you for reading, and happy Mac hacking!

 Got a favorite trick from this book? Let me know in your review!

Effortless MacBook Mastery: Lazy Tricks & Smart Shortcuts for Maximum Productivity
Unlock the true power of your MacBook and work smarter—not harder!
Are you using your MacBook to its full potential, or are you stuck in time-consuming
tasks that could be done in seconds? Effortless MacBook Mastery is the ultimate guide
for anyone who wants to maximize productivity, automate tasks, and simplify their
workflow using smart tricks and hidden features.
What You'll Learn in This Book:
Time-Saving Keyboard Shortcuts – Navigate and control your Mac like a pro.
Spotlight & Siri Hacks – Find files, launch apps, and get things done faster.
AirDrop & Handoff Secrets – Instantly transfer files between Apple devices.
Mission Control & Multi-Desktop Mastery – Organize your workspace effortlessly.
Finder & File Management Tricks – Never lose a file again with smart organization.
Performance & Maintenance Hacks – Keep your Mac running fast and smooth.
Bonus: Automation with Shortcuts & AppleScript – Let your Mac do the work for you!
Why This Book?
Perfect for beginners and experienced Mac users – Learn both basic and advanced
tricks.
No technical jargon – Simple, step-by-step instructions.
Boost efficiency instantly – Implement these tips today and see the difference.
Designed for busy people – Work smarter in less time.
If you love efficiency, productivity, and getting the most out of your MacBook, this
book is for you. Whether you're a student, professional, entrepreneur, or casual user,
these lazy tricks will make your Mac experience effortless and enjoyable.
Get your copy now and start mastering your MacBook today!

ISBN 9798315570547

90000

9 798315 570547